A Brief History of

PALESTINE

ISMAIL ADAM PATEL

AL-AQSA PUBLISHERS

© Al-Aqsa Publishers, January 2023

Published by
AL-AQSA PUBLISHERS
101C Gwendolen Road
Leicester, LE5 5FL, UK
Tel: (0116) 212 5441
Website: www.foa.org.uk
Email: info@foa.org.uk

ISBN 978-1-7391310-1-2

British Library Cataloguing in Publication Data

Patel, Ismail Adam
      Palestine : brief history
      1. Arab-Israeli conflict
      2. Palestine - History
      I. Title
      956.9'405

Cover design and typeset by: Shoayb Adam

Cover Artwork by David Roberts 1842 Copy-right Alamy Limited

Contents

List of Illustrations

Images

Preface

Palestine has been the focus of conflict for several decades, so much so that many people have grown accustomed to the daily reports of misery from the region that appear in print, broadcast and online media. In typical examples of 'mediation', the news is often tailored in a way that is favourable to one side prior to being released to the public. In this way, the protagonists have been successful in shaping minds, moulding emotions and eliciting desired reactions. In the West it is generally the Israeli version of events that is widely accepted; this was especially so in the early years of what has become known as the Palestinian conflict. The reason for this acceptance is an efficient propaganda machine that depicts Israel as the only democracy in the Middle East, and therefore comparable to European states in terms of culture and the challenges it faces in the 'war on terror'.

The Palestinians have to combat many factors, including a pro-Israel historical account of the conflict which delegitimises the Palestinian struggle while whitewashing Israeli crimes and depicting the 1948 war as a legitimate war of independence, rather than a belligerent war of ethnic cleansing and occupation. However, in recent years there has been a noticeable shift in perspective and a growing awareness of the Palestinian struggle that is leading to a review of the popular Western understanding of the conflict. The dominant historic accounts are now being challenged worldwide, and even from within Israel itself. At the forefront of the revision of Palestine–Israel history are leading Israeli historians, often referred to as 'new historians', such as Ilan Pappé and the late Israel Shahak. As a result, it is now becoming possible, at least in academic circles, to challenge the Zionist interpretation and claims about the Palestine–Israel situation without being labelled anti-Semitic.

This book aims to introduce readers to the Palestinian conflict in a fair and holistic fashion by tracing events from the earliest history of the region to the present day. To objectively assess the crisis and envisage a better future, the past needs to be understood; the intention of A Brief History of Palestine is to present the reader with a narrative that challenges the widely promoted version of events. This journey across the centuries includes ancient history, the religious traditions associated with the land, the founding of Israel, and modern political tensions. It is hoped that this book will not only inform its readers but spur them towards working for justice in the Holy Land.

December 2022

Introduction

The Middle East

Palestine—home to numerous prophets—has been in the hearts and minds of people around the globe for centuries. Many people, cultures and civilisations made Palestine their home and left their mark on the land. Mostly living a peaceful and prosperous life, conflict in the Holy Land generally only occurred when invaders made exclusive claims to it. This happened in 1099 CE, during the Crusades, and is happening once more as successive Israeli governments have striven to rewrite Palestine's history and deprive its indigenous people of their rightful claims to peace and equality.

In bygone times, Palestine attracted seekers of peace and solace including Muslim, Christian and Jewish pilgrims. Today it is a land of occupation and oppression; discrimination has transformed what was once a pluralistic society into a land of apartheid, where people are segregated according to creed and culture.

While this book is not an encyclopaedic account of Palestinian history, nor a record of every event or incident, significant episodes have been covered to equip readers with a sound general knowledge of the region's history. *A Brief History of Palestine* aims to introduce readers to the story behind Palestine and demonstrate how this area, once a peaceful and serene part of the world, has become synonymous with discord and human misery.

CHAPTER 1

The Ancient Civilisations
10,000-586 BCE

Jerusalem: The Stone Age city

1.1 The ruins of Jericho

10,000 BC

The city of Jericho was founded around 12,000 years ago and is today located in the West Bank. The ancient city covered around 4 hectares (10 acres) and archaeological evidence indicates that it was initially built by the Natufians, the ancestors of the Arabs.

8000 BCE

Researchers believe that excavations in Jerusalem by archaeologists Kathleen Kenyon in the 1960s and Yigal Shiloh in the 1970s prove that the city had been fortified 8,000 years before Jesus (peace be upon him). A three-metre thick wall re-enforced with supporting stone towers was discovered in the 1970s, protecting the city in general and in particular the area overlooking the city's invaluable water spring. Because the east side of the old city was very steep, a group of *mastabas* (Arabic for stone benches) had been constructed for people to use for rest; some believe that the stone benches could be the ones referred to in the Bible as mellos which are said to have been built by David (Dawud) and later repaired by Solomon (Sulayman) and Ezekiel (Dhul-Kifl) (peace be upon them).

1.2 The Tower of Jericho

5000-4000 BCE

According to the *Encyclopaedia Britannica*, during the fifth millennium BCE Palestine may have been developing more rapidly than any other area in the world at the time. Many peoples, such as the Ghassulians, were immigrating into Palestine and developing permanent villages and efficient agricultural techniques. Copper and flint industries were developing, and there was evidence of ivory working, suggesting the emergence of specialist artisans.

Archaeological evidence suggests that Jerusalem has been inhabited since the fourth millennium BCE, around the time people began to immigrate into the region. Evidence of pottery and rooms constructed in natural rock support this view.

1.3 The Tell el-Amarna letters

3000 BCE

The Canaanites, who migrated from the area that today comprises Syria and Lebanon, began occupying present-day Palestine in 3000 BCE. The Canaanites invented the linear alphabet that we use today, and by extension the written word culture that became the basis of the Western writing system. The Canaanites were also Semites and some spoke Hebrew.

Jerusalem is first mentioned as a Canaanite city around 3000 BCE, in a letter from the Pharaoh of Egypt to one of his governors. These letters, written on clay tablets, are called the Egyptian Tell-el-Amarna letters. Since 1887, over 400 such tablets have been discovered. They provide details of the communication between the Pharaoh and the vassal princes of Palestine and Syria.

2000 BCE

By around 4500 BCE, the land situated a few hundred kilometres to the east of Canaan, between the rivers Tigris and Euphrates in present day Iraq, was inhabited. The area that developed was called Sumer, and the capital of the region was Ur. The Sumerians left hundreds of records by way of clay tablets on which they used to write messages. Around 2370 BCE, a Semite from the north west of Sumer called Sargon of Akkad (Agade) attacked and conquered Sumer, which he then

ruled for 54 years. Upon his death, the Sumerians reoccupied their land and the city of Ur flourished once again.

A few centuries later, around 2000 BCE, another Semite group called the Amorites occupied Sumer and looted Ur. The Amorites' reign came to an end in around 1790 BCE, when Hammurabi of Babylon captured Sumer. Babylonian rule over the region remained uncontested for the next few hundred years.

It was during this period that the Prophet Abraham (Ibrahim) was born in Ur. Abraham's teachings against idolatry were in conflict to the traditions of his family and community; with his life in danger Abraham, his wife and nephew Lot (Lut) migrated to Canaan.

The religious dimension

The Prophet Abraham settled in Jerusalem and frequently visited neighbouring lands. Abraham's first son, Ishmael (Ismail), settled in Arabia while his second son, Isaac (Ishaq), succeeded him in Palestine. Isaac was the father of Jacob (Yaqub, also known as Israel), whose son Joseph (Yusuf) settled in Egypt. Joseph later called his father and brothers to Egypt, where they lived and increased in number.

> ### Al 'Imran, 3:67
> Ibrahim was neither a Jew nor a Christian, but he was a Muslim wholly devoted to God. And he joined no gods with Allah.

> ### Islam
> Abraham left his older son Ishmael in Makkah, where they later rebuilt the Kaaba together. With his other son, Isaac, Abraham rebuilt another house of worship, Al-Aqsa mosque in Jerusalem.
>
> ### Christianity
> Abraham built altars (places of worship) wherever he had Theophany (i.e. he talked to or saw God). These places include Nablus, Bethel, Hebron and Moriah.
>
> (*Genesis* 12: 7, 8; 13: 18; 22: 9)

1500 BCE

A few hundred years later, Palestine fell under Egyptian rule. The Pharaoh of the time oppressed and enslaved a number of Abraham's descendants (via his son Isaac) who had settled in Egypt.

Moses

Moses (Musa) was also one of God's prophets and he tried to convince Pharaoh that his actions were oppressive and wrong. Pharaoh rejected the message and began persecuting those following Moses. Moses led his followers, the Children of Israel (so called because they were descendants of the Prophet Yaqub), from Egypt towards Palestine.

In the darkness of the night, Moses and his followers headed towards the Red Sea with Pharaoh and his army in pursuit. When they saw the sea before them and the army gaining ground behind them, the Israelites were convinced they were doomed. It was at this moment of distress that Moses turned to God and was instructed to strike the water with his staff. On doing so, the sea parted with the crests of the waves standing like two mountains on either side of a path through the water.

66

And when they reached the sea, God commanded...Lift up thy rod and stretch out thine hand over the sea and divide it and the Children of Israel shall go on dry ground through the midst of the sea.
(*Exodus* 14: 16)

99

Moses led his people through the parted water, but as Pharaoh followed in pursuit, God commanded the sea to return to its natural state. Pharaoh and his men were drowned and the Israelites were saved.

Instead of being thankful, the Israelites were ungrateful:

> And they said unto Moses, because there were no graves in Egypt, hast thou taken us away to die in the wilderness? Wherefore hast thou dealt thus with us, to carry us forth out of Egypt?
> (*Exodus* 14: 11)
>
> Is not this the word that we did tell thee in Egypt, saying let us alone, that we may serve the Egyptians? For it had been better for us to serve the Egyptians than that we should die in the wilderness.
> (*Exodus* 14: 12)

God instructed Moses to lead his followers to the Holy Land (Palestine) that had been promised to Abraham as the place where the pious and God-fearing from among his descendants would live to uphold God's sacred laws.

However, the Children of Israel were ungrateful and cowardly, and when Moses ordered them to fight the Canaanites, who were the inhabitants of Palestine at the time, they refused. The Israelites argued that the Canaanites were of mighty strength and power, and that they would not go further unless the Canaanites left voluntarily:

> They said: 'O Musa! In it (this holy land) are a people of great strength, and we shall never enter it until they leave it; when they leave then we will enter'.
> (*al-Ma'idah* 5: 25)

Despite Moses's best efforts to persuade the Israelites to enter Palestine, they refused to listen. Instead, they told Moses to go alone with his Lord:

> **"**
>
> They said: 'O Musa! We shall never enter it as long as they are there. So go, you and your Lord, and fight; we are sitting right here'.
>
> (*al-Ma'idah* 5: 26)
>
> **"**

After the Israelites' rebellion, God punished them by banishing them to wander in the desert for 40 years. Moses never reached Palestine and died in the wilderness.

Meanwhile in Greece

The Greek civilisation collapsed around 1200 BCE , during the course of the ten-year Trojan War, and as a result of this collapse many communities took to the sea as pirates. One of these communities was the Philistines, who established themselves on the coast of Canaan – Palestine.

David

Some time later, the Israelites united under King Saul (Talut) and battled with the Philistines. The Bible speaks of Goliath, the giant of the Philistines, challenging the Israelites to single combat. However, it was not King Saul who confronted Goliath but a little shepherd boy called David (Dawud). The story of how David, armed with only a sling, brought down the mighty Goliath is well known.

> **"**
>
> And there went out a champion out of the camp of the Philistines, named Goliath of Gath whose height was six cubits and a span. And he had a helmet of brass upon his head and he was armed with a coat of mail and the weight of the coat was 5,000 shekels of brass. And he had Greaves of brass upon his legs and a target of brass between his shoulders. And the staff of his spear was like a weaver's beam...
>
> (*1 Samuel* 17: 4–7)
>
> **"**

> 66
>
> And David put his hand in his bag and took out a stone and
> slung it, which smote the Philistine in his forehead, and he fell
> upon his face to the Earth.
>
> (*1 Samuel* 17: 49)
>
> 99

Saul was the first king of the Israelites. However, following David's victory he became jealous of David and attempted to get rid of him. David retreated to the wilderness with some companions and formed a coalition with the Israelites' old enemies: the Philistines. The coalition then attacked and killed Saul.

David was crowned the second King of the Israelites. As king he united his men and moved towards Jerusalem, which had been ruled by the Jebusites, a Canaanite tribe, for around 500 years. David defeated the Jebusites and Jerusalem became the capital city of his kingdom. King David lived together with the local population and did not kill or expel the Jebusites; a fact which is also mentioned in the Bible:

> 66
>
> The Jebusites dwell with the children of Judaea
> at Jerusalem unto this day.
>
> (*Joshua* 15: 63)
>
> 99

According to Jewish traditions cited in the Aggadah, David's mother was a daughter of Ithra, an Ishmaelite (Ishmael was the elder son of Abraham). King David himself had three wives: Michal, the daughter of King Saul; Maacah, the daughter of the Canaanite King Talmai of Geshur; and Bathsheba, a Canaanite from Giloh. Bathsheba was Solomon's mother.

David united the different Jewish tribes with great difficulty, and pacified other citizens. His reign lasted only 40 years, from 1018–978 BCE.

> **Old Testament**
>
> King David was commanded by God to build an altar. David complied and purchased land from Ornan (Araunah), the Jebusite and began to build. David died before the altar was completed, but this land was where David's son, Solomon, would build his temple.
>
> (*2 Chronicles* 3: 1)

Solomon

After David's death, his son Solomon ruled over the kingdom for a further 40 years from 978–938 BCE. It was during this period that Solomon completed the temple his father had begun. After Solomon's death his son Rehoboam was crowned, but within a very short period of time there was a revolt, and enmity between the different Jewish tribes created divisions once more. By 922 BCE, the kingdom had split into two: the North became Israel (later called Samaria) and the South became Judea, with Jerusalem as its capital.

> **The split**
>
> Ten of the 12 Jewish tribes moved to the Northern Kingdom and only two tribes were in the South, with Jerusalem as its capital.

The two neighbouring kingdoms became rivals. The great powers of the time took advantage of this rivalry and in 722 BCE the Assyrians conquered Israel.

> **Islam**
>
> According to Muslim scholars, Prophet Adam built the first house of worship in Jerusalem, the Al-Aqsa mosque, 40 years after he built the Kaaba in Makkah. Prophet Abraham later rebuilt the Al-Aqsa mosque with his son, Isaac. Prophet David began building it once again during his rule, a venture that the Prophet Solomon then completed.
>
> **Judaism**
>
> Jewish attachment to the 'Temple' begins with Solomon. Jews believe it was Solomon who built the first house in Jerusalem to remember God.

After a time Judea descended into corruption, idolatry and superstition. As the Jewish tribes slipped into idolatry, a prophet called Jeremiah (Aramiah) warned them of divine punishment if they failed to correct their ways. Instead of heeding his advice, Jeremiah was imprisoned.

66

> They … returned to their evil ways, erected altars and high places on every hill and under every green tree. In Judea there were as many gods as there were towns … Images of gold and silver, of wood and stone, were again erected in the houses. The Temple itself was … once more desecrated by hideous idols.
>
> (Graetz, *History of the Jews*, vol. 1, p. 300)

99

In 586 BCE, a calamity befell Judea and Jerusalem. Nebuchadnezzar, the king of Babylon, attacked Judea and laid it to waste. This episode is mentioned in the Quran, which states that his army was mighty and entered the 'innermost parts of their houses'. Nebuchadnezzar destroyed the Temple and took Jerusalem's surviving population to Babylon.

Summary

A united kingdom of Israel lasted for 90 years, from 1020–922 BCE. In 922 BCE the kingdom split into:

Israel

The northern kingdom, which lasted for 200 years, from 922–722 BCE

Judea

The southern kingdom, which lasted for 336 years, from 922–586 BCE.

This Marks the end of Jewish Rule in Palestine

CHAPTER 2

The Ancient Superpowers
586 BCE-70 CE

The Babylonians

When Nebuchadnezzar, the king of Babylon, took control of Judea in 586 BCE, the Babylonians destroyed almost everything, including the Temple. Jerusalem itself was reduced to rubble and Judea ceased to exist as a kingdom.

The Persians

The emergence of the Persian Empire to the east of Babylon, under the leadership of Shah Cyrus, led to the attack and occupation of Babylon in around 550 BCE. All of the Babylonian-ruled territories were subsequently conquered, including Canaan and Jerusalem.

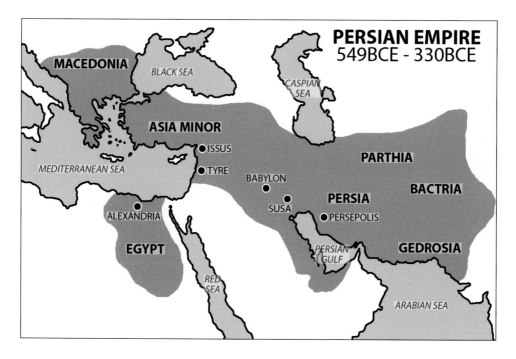

Sympathetic to the Jews, the Persians allowed them to return to Jerusalem. Some returned, but others chose to stay in the more fertile lands of Persia. When Darius was later crowned King of Persia, he not only permitted the rebuilding of the Temple in Jerusalem, but also provided financial assistance. The construction of the second Temple began around 538 BCE. Persian rule ended after 200 years, in 330 BCE, following the invasion by Alexander the Great.

Alexander the Great

Alexander III of Macedon—also known as Alexander the Great—was born in 356 BCE. On the death of his father, Philip II, Alexander set out to conquer the world; he was 15 at the time. Travelling east, he first encountered the Persians led by Darius III on the battlefield at Issus in 333 BCE. After gaining victory over Darius, Alexander moved on to conquer Tyre and Jerusalem. He then conquered Egypt and Babylon.

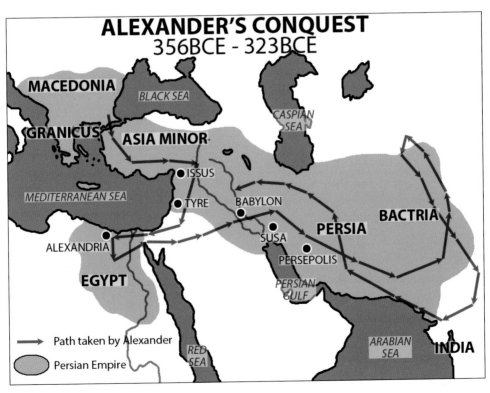

Alexander did not live to see the fruits of his labours. Having marched 11,000 miles with his soldiers and conquered vast territories, he wished to continue but turned back because his soldiers were growing homesick. As he and his armies were en route to Macedonia, Alexander contracted a severe fever that led to his untimely death in Babylon in 323 BCE, at the age of 32.

Alexander's early death resulted in a power vacuum that caused his empire to fracture. The Ptolemies took charge of Egypt and the Seleucids took control of an area that roughly comprises of present-day Palestine, Syria, Jordan and Iraq. Although Alexander's empire was divided, Hellenism triumphed throughout. Greek became dominant and even the Torah was translated into Greek. This is how the famous translation of the Old Testament, called the Septuagint, came into existence.

The mix of Eastern and Western civilisations resulting from Alexander's conquests led to the emergence of a new civilisation and culture called Hellenism. Hellenism survived for over 300 years, during which the Middle East and the other regions that Alexander occupied not only enjoyed the best of Greek culture, language and education, but also absorbed some of these characteristics into the respective local cultures.

Greek culture was strong in Canaan, and so the Jews and Canaanites fell under its influence. Greek colonies were established in Gaza and around the central plain of Palestine. Hellenisation was so complete that a statue of the Greek god Jupiter was placed on the altar of the Temple in Jerusalem and sacrifices were offered to it. However, after several years of assimilation into Greco culture and thought, the Hasmonean Jews rebelled in what came to be known as the Maccabean Revolt. This was an uprising against the Seleucids and saw the Maccabees, as the Jewish rebels were known, recapture Jerusalem in 164 BCE. After conquering the city, the rebels began fighting internally over who should rule. In 88 BCE the Pharisees faction of Jews rebelled and captured Jerusalem from the Hasmoneans; but their lack of unity meant that they could not retain power. Another Jewish sect of the Pharisees then tried to confront the Hasmoneans.

As the Jews remained engaged in internal conflict, a new and mighty empire was emerging in the West: the Romans.

Roman rule

2.1 The ruins of Carthage, Tunisia

As Hellenism waned, the Roman Empire expanded its territories and influence. Roman legions crushed Carthage and took control of the Mediterranean Sea in the Punic Wars of 264 BCE. Then they turned east; under the orders of the Roman Emperor Pompey, the Romans conquered Jerusalem in 63 BCE. So began a new chapter in the city's history.

> **"**
>
> I came, I saw, I conquered.
>
> Julius Caesar
>
> **"**

Palestine and its surrounding territories were divided into Roman provinces with appointed procurators to take charge of day-to-day affairs, on behalf of Rome. The procurators, who were responsible for paying taxes to Rome, oppressed the general public. Herod, a descendant of the Edomite tribe, had recently converted to Judaism and was appointed to oversee Jerusalem. Like other procurators, Herod was loyal to Rome and this ensured that he remained protected during his reign from 37–4 BCE.

During his reign, Herod extended the Temple on a grand scale and placed a golden eagle at its entrance to please the Romans. This act was seen as heresy by religious Jews. (*Encyclopaedia Judaica*, vol. 2, p. 493).

Myth

Nowadays, some Jews claim that the Buraq Wall—also known as the 'Wailing Wall' or the 'Western Wall', and which is an integral part of the western boundary wall of the Noble Sanctuary of Al-Aqsa, is all that remains of Herod's Temple.

Reality

2.2 The Wailing Wall, Jerusalem

A League of Nations Commission undertook a two-year study and reported the following in 1931:
'To the Muslims belong the sole ownership of, and the sole proprietary right to, the Western Wall, seeing that it forms an integral part of Al Aqsa sanctuary, which is Waqf property. To the Muslims there also belongs the ownership of the pavement in front of the wall and of the adjacent so-called Maghribi quarters opposite the wall, in as much as the last mentioned property was made Waqf under Muslim Sharia law, it is being dedicated to charitable purposes'.

(Walid Khalidi, *Before their Diaspora*, p.90)

After Herod's death, the area under his rule was divided among his three sons: Archelaus, Antipas, and Philip. This changed after 44 CE, when all of Palestine became a Roman state.

Jesus

Both Christians and Muslims believe in the miraculous birth of Prophet Jesus (Isa), as being born without a father. Judaism rejects this and does not consider Jesus as a prophet. Mary (Maryam), the mother of Jesus was a Palestinian from Nazareth, and even today Christians in the Middle East are known as Nazarenes.

Islam

She said, 'O my Lord! How shall I have a son when no man has touched me?' He said, 'Even so, Allah creates what He wills. When He has decreed a matter, He but says to it, "Be" and it is!'

(*Al 'Imran* 3:47)

Christianity

An Angel came to Mary and said, 'Behold, thou shall conceive a son and call him Jesus. And the Lord shall give unto him the throne of his father David: And he shall reign over the house of Jacob forever'.

(*Luke* 1: 28–33)

Judaism

Judaism rejects Jesus as a prophet.

The Bible

Jesus foretold the destruction of the Temple: 'And Jesus went out and departed from the temple and his disciples came to him for to show him the buildings of the Temple. And Jesus said unto them, seeing all these things. "Verily I say unto you there shall not be left here one stone upon another that shall not be thrown down".

(*Matthew* 24: 1–2)

2.3 The earliest map of Jerusalem (6th Century)

2.4 Via Dolorosa, Jerusalem

The Jewish high priest at the time was a man called Caiaphas, who called a meeting of leading Jews to develop a strategy to get rid of Jesus. According to the Bible, it was during this meeting when one of Jesus's disciples, Judas Iscariot, came to them and asked, 'What will you give me if I deliver him (Jesus) to you?' He bargained with them until they agreed to give him 30 pieces of silver known as shekels. Thus, the plot was laid for Jesus's capture. However, only the Roman governor, Pontius Pilate, could condemn people to death so a group of Jews went to him and demanded Jesus's arrest, trial and execution.

> ### The Gospel of St Matthew states
> Pilate said unto them, 'What shall I do with Jesus which is called Christ?' They all said unto him, 'Let him be crucified'. And the governor said, 'Why, what evil has he done?' But they cried out the more, saying, 'Let him be crucified'. When Pilate saw that he could prevail nothing, but rather a tumult was made, he took water and washed his hands before the multitude, saying, 'I am innocent of the blood of this just person: see you to it'. Then answered all the people and said, 'His blood be on us and our children'.
>
> (Matthew 27: 22–25)

When Jesus found disbelief on their part he said:

66

'Who will be my helpers (in the work of Allah)?' Said the disciples: 'We are Allah's helpers, we believe in Allah and do bear witness that we are Muslims. Our Lord! We believe in what You have revealed and we follow the messenger. Then write us down as those who bear witness. And (those who rejected) plotted and planned and Allah too planned, and the best of planners is Allah'.
(Al 'Imran 3: 52–54)

99

Christians believe that Jesus was crucified on the cross, but the Holy Quran denies this and says that Allah replaced him with another person whose appearance was similar to that of Jesus. Allah then raised Jesus up to the heavens.

> That they said (in boast), we killed Isa, son of Mary, the messenger
> of Allah. But they killed him not, nor crucified him. Only a likeness
> of that was shown to them. And those who differ therein are full of
> doubts, with no knowledge, but only conjecture to follow, for a
> surety they killed him not. Nay, Allah raised him unto Himself,
> and Allah is exalted in Power, Wise.
>
> (*al-Nisa'* 4: 157–158)

During Jesus' lifetime, Palestine's population was a mixture of Jews, Sabeans, Pagans and Romans.

Revolt against the Romans

In May 66 CE Palestine was aflame; a revolt against the Romans had broken out resulting in many Romans and their collaborators (mainly Jewish priests) being put to death (Josephus, *The Jewish War*, p. 332). Rome sent General Vespasian with his son, Titus, as second-in-command, at the head of an army to put down the revolt and confront the Palestinian forces. These forces consisted of non-Jewish Jerusalemites, Edomites and some Jewish Israelites. Historians estimate that the Jews made up around 14 per cent of the total force resisting Roman power.

After several months of fighting, Vespasian and Titus crushed the rebellion and drove the remaining rebels and thousands of refugees to Jerusalem. In the spring and summer of 70 CE, Titus laid siege to Jerusalem and put down the final elements of the revolt, flattening the city in its entirety, including Herod's Temple. The few remaining Jews were exiled from Palestine and forbidden from entering the Holy City.

> **This marks the end of the Jewish presence in Jerusalem.**

CHAPTER 3

Christian Palestine
70-634 CE

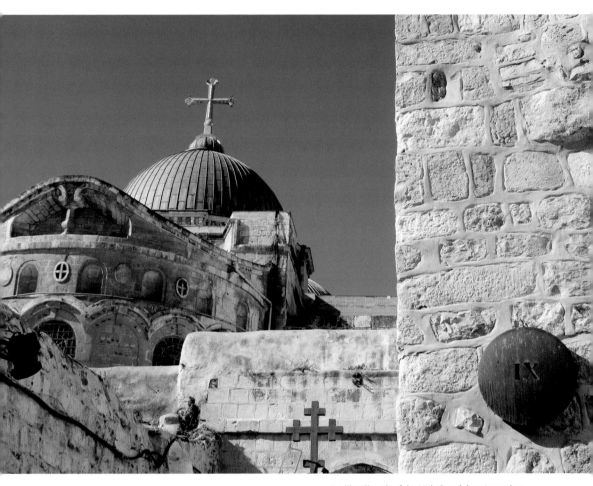

3.1 The Church of the Holy Sepulchre, Jerusalem

After Jesus's ascension, his teachings spread far and wide, both among Roman citizens and the communities which the Romans ruled. The Roman authorities, however, viewed the belief system that later became known as Christianity as a threat and banned it. Christians were persecuted throughout the Empire and it became difficult to practise and proclaim the faith openly.

When the Roman Empire became too large and cumbersome, the Emperor Diocletian decided to divide it into two: the Western Empire and the Eastern Empire. The capital of the Western Empire was in Rome whereas the capital of the Eastern Empire was in Byzantium. The Emperor Constantine renamed Byzantium 'Constantinople' (which is now called Istanbul), and the Eastern Roman Empire became known as the Byzantine Empire.

By 320 CE the Roman Emperor Constantine embraced Christianity; this not only saved Christians within the Empire from persecution, but also helped the faith spread further afield as the Empire's official religion. Under Christianity, Palestine's economy, especially Jerusalem, benefitted greatly. Wealthy Romans constructed churches in the city, which attracted pilgrims and businessmen. However, for Jews things went from bad to worse:

> **"**
>
> Christianity had made itself master of Judea, and had become the heir of Judaism...Jerusalem had ceased to be a centre for the Jews, it had become a thoroughly Christian city...The law forbidding Jews to enter the holy city, which had been revived by Constantine, was, after the death of Julian, most rigorously enforced by the authorities ...
>
> (Graetz, *History of the Jews*, vol. 3, pp 11–12)
>
> **"**

> Palestine remained under Christian rule for 294 years (until 614 CE).

A Christian massacre

After almost 300 years of Christian rule, the Roman Empire began to split into different religious factions, which resulted in an overall weakening of its defences. The neighbouring Persian Empire exploited this weakness by attacking and occupying large parts of Roman territory.

> **The Persian Empire**
> Included modern day Iraq, Iran, Afghanistan and Pakistan.

As the Persians approached Jerusalem in 614 CE, they found the Jews to be loyal allies who not only welcomed them to escape Christian oppression, but also assisted them in the destruction of churches and slaying of Christians. Many Jews bought Christians and then killed them; around 90,000 Christians were murdered at the hands of Jews in Jerusalem alone. A Christian monk, Antiochus Strategos, provides a contemporary account of the Persian capture of Jerusalem:

> 66
>
> The evil foemen entered the city in great fury, like infuriated beasts and irritated serpents. They slew all whom they found. Like mad dogs they tore with their teeth the flesh of the faithful, and respected none at all, neither male nor female, neither young nor old, neither child nor baby, neither priest nor monk, neither virgin nor widow... They listened not to appeals of supplicants...On the contrary they destroyed persons of every age, massacred them like animals, cut them in pieces, mowed sundry of them down like cabbages, so that all alike had severally to drain the cup full of bitterness. Lamentation and terror might be seen in Jerusalem. Holy churches were burned with fire, others were demolished, majestic altars fell prone, sacred crosses were trampled underfoot, life-giving icons were spat upon by the unclean. Then their wrath fell upon priests and deacons: they slew them in their churches like dumb animals.
>
> (Geanakoplos, *Byzantium*, p. 266)
>
> 99

Jerusalem's patriarch, Zacharias, was taken to Persia as a prisoner — along with 35,000 Christians and the fragment of the 'True Cross' from the Church of the Holy Sepulchre. Whatever the Persians did not destroy during the invasion was razed to the ground, including the Church of the Resurrection (Avi-Yonah, *A History of the Holy Land*, p. 181).

A short time later, the Persians allowed Christians to practise their faith again, and under the leadership of Modestus most churches and holy sites were renovated, with the pace gaining momentum after the victory of Byzantine emperor Heraclius over the Persians in 627 CE.

> ### Persian Rule in Palestine
> The Persian Empire ruled Jerusalem for eight years—from 614 to 622 CE—and thereafter only with dwindling influence until 627 CE.

After his victory over the Persians, a triumphant Heraclius personally returned the fragment of the 'True Cross' to Jerusalem on 21 March 630 CE. However, Heraclius's victory was disastrous for the Jews. They were banished from Jerusalem and ordered not to come within 5 kilometres of the Holy City (Turtledove, *The Chronicles of Theophanes*). According to Butler (*The Arab Conquest of Egypt*, p. 134), the adversity of exile from Jerusalem for the Jews was the least of their worries compared to the edict that followed, instructing provinces throughout the Empire to persecute them and resulting in 'something like a general massacre of the Jews'.

Modestus, a veteran of the Persian years, was appointed interim Patriarch for Jerusalem after Zacharias was taken by the Persians. In 630 CE, he succeeded Zacharias as Jerusalem's Patriarch in his own right. He died in 634 CE and was replaced by Sophronius.

CHAPTER 4

Islamic Palestine
635-1094

Muslims follow Islam, which literally means surrendering one's own will to that of God (Allah). Muslims accept Islam through the Islamic declaration of faith, the *shahadah*: 'There is no god except Allah; Muhammad is the messenger of Allah'. Muslims believe that all of God's messengers from the beginning of time have literally been Muslims (i.e. they have submitted themselves to the will of God), though Islam as we know it today was presented to the Prophet Muhammad (peace be upon him) by revelation. The words of God that the Prophet received were transcribed into a book of guidance that all Muslims follow, and that book is the Quran:

> **"**
>
> This day I have perfected for you your religion, and have bestowed upon you My Bounty in full measure, and have been pleased to assign for you Islam as your religion.
>
> (*al-Ma'idah* 5: 3)
>
> **"**

> ### The Semites
> The Arabs are a Semitic people; they are ethnically and linguistically related to the northern Semitic tribe from which emerged the Canaanites and the Hebrews.

> **"**
>
> The First Commandment, 'Thou shalt have no other gods but Me' and 'Hear, O Israel, the Lord thy God is One'.
>
> (*Deuteronomy* 5: 7 and 6)
>
> **"**

In this sense, the Quran is often referred to as God's final testament.

The spread of Islam

Following the liberation of Makkah during the Prophet Muhammed's life, Islam gained great momentum and the faith spread far and wide. By 637 CE, within five years of the Prophet Muhammad's passing, Muslims had control of most of al-Sham (the region of modern-day Syria, Jordan, Lebanon and Palestine) and were at the gates of Jerusalem. In the east, Muslims swept through Iraq and Iran, the land ruled by the Persians.

> **The importance of Jerusalem to Muslims**
> o   Jerusalem is referred to 82 times, directly and indirectly, in the Holy Quran.
> o   The area has been 'blessed' by God for all of His creation.
> o   Al-Aqsa, in Jerusalem, is believed to be the second house of God; built soon after the Kaaba in Makkah.
> o   There are many ahadith (sayings of the Prophet Muhammad) that exalt and sanctify Jerusalem.
> o   The reward for praying in the mosque of Al-Aqsa is 500 times greater than in other mosques, apart from the Haram in Makkah and the Prophet's Mosque in Madinah.
> o   It was from the precincts of Al-Aqsa in Jerusalem that the Prophet Muhammed made the miraculous journey of Al-Miraj (ascension to heaven).
> o   Muslims originally faced Jerusalem during their prayers whilst they resided in Makkah (before the Prophet migrated to Madinah) and for 16–17 months after the Prophet Muhammed's migration to Madinah.
> o   Muslims are advised to make a journey to Jerusalem for the sole purpose of performing *salah* (prayer) in Al-Aqsa.
> o   Giving a gift of oil to be burnt in the blessed mosque of Al-Aqsa in Jerusalem is equivalent to the reward of performing *salah* there.

It was during the time of the second Caliph (the Prophet Muhammed's successor as leader of the Muslims), 'Umar ibn al-Khattab that the Muslim army arrived at the gates of Jerusalem. The city's Christian inhabitants locked themselves in and agreed to surrender only if 'Umar, who was in Madinah at the time, personally took possession of the city's keys. Though the Muslim army was capable of taking the city by force, they agreed to the request with a view of minimising casualties. As a result, 'Umar travelled from Madinah to Jerusalem where Sophronius, the Patriarch of Jerusalem, made him sign a treaty in which he was also requested to exclude Jews from living within the city.

4.1 Al-Aqsa Sanctuary, also known as Masjid Al-Aqsa

'Umar entered the city on foot, without shedding blood or harassing its inhabitants. Once inside, he asked Sophronious to take him to the Al-Aqsa sanctuary. When they reached the Noble Sanctuary, 'Umar was shocked to find it covered in litter as the Romans had been using the area as a refuse tip. The Caliph immediately knelt down and began to clear the area with his own hands. When the Muslims saw what he was doing, they followed suit and soon the entire area of approximately 14 hectares (35 acres), was cleaned. 'Umar commissioned the construction of a wooden mosque on the southern end of the Noble Sanctuary where the present-day black domed mosque of Al-Aqsa stands.

After the Muslims had liberated Jerusalem and the rest of al-Sham, the prime benefactors of this liberation were the Jewish people. For the first time in 500 years, since their expulsion from the Holy Land, the Jews were allowed to live and practise their religion freely in the vicinity of Jerusalem.

> **The Jews return**
> After the Muslim conquest of Jerusalem, 70 Jewish families took up residence there.
>
> *(Encyclopaedia Judaica)*

Umar's Assurance

In the name of Allah, The Most Merciful, the Most Compassionate.

This is the assurance of safety, which the servant of Allah, 'Umar ibn al-Khattab, the Commander of the Faithful, has granted to the people of Jerusalem.

He has granted them safety for their lives and possessions, their churches and crosses, the sick and the healthy of the city, and for the rest of its religious community. Their churches will not be inhabited nor destroyed. Neither they, nor the land on which they stand, nor their crosses, nor their possessions will be confiscated. They will not be forcibly converted, nor any one of them harmed. No Jew will live with them in Jerusalem.

The people of Jerusalem must pay the poll tax, like the people of the other cities, and they must expel the Romans and the robbers.

As for those who wish to leave, their lives and possessions shall be safeguarded until they reach their place of safety, and as for those who remain they will be safe. Those people of Jerusalem who wish to leave with the Romans, take their possessions and abandon their churches and crosses will be safe until they reach their place of safety.

These assurances under the covenant of Allah are the responsibility of His Prophet, of the Caliphs and the faithful if the people of Jerusalem pay the poll tax according to their obligations.

The Golden Age

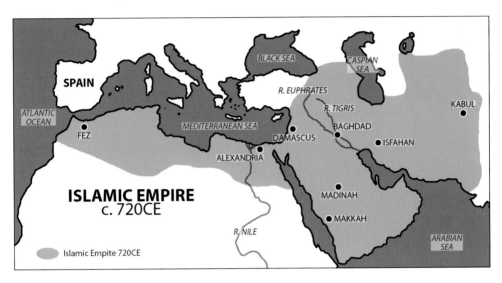

After the spread of Islam from India in the east to Spain in the west, Muslims consolidated their position, resulting in a cultural and educational revolution. The major cities of the Islamic world including Jerusalem, Baghdad, Damascus, Isfahan, Fez, Cairo and Cordoba became intellectual centres of learning, research and debate.

Some of the world's greatest philosophers, scientists, surgeons, architects, historians, geographers, poets, writers and adventurers emerged. This intellectual and scientific renaissance was not only the preserve of Muslims; many great Jewish intellectuals also benefitted from the tolerance of Islamic rule.

> ### Jewish scholars
> Famous Jewish personalities during the Golden Age included:
> o   Maimonides
> o   Abraham ibn Daud
> o   Judah ben Samuel Ha-Levi

In the sciences, Islamic intellectuals and scientists developed great advances in the field of scientific investigation.

> After materia medica, astronomy and mathematics the Arabs made their greatest scientific contribution in chemistry. In the study of chemistry and other physical sciences the Arabs introduced the objective experiment, a decided improvement over the hazy speculation of the Greeks. Accurate in the observation of phenomena and diligent in the accumulation of facts …
>
> (*The History of the Arabs*, Philip K. Hitti, p. 380)

In the Islamic world, some great scholars included:

4.2 An early Arab distillation device

Chemistry

Jabir ibn Hayyan (c. 776) of Kofa is known as the father of modern chemistry. Jabir wrote more than 100 works and is credited for advancing the theory of geological formation of metals and the 'sulphur-mercury theory' of metallic composition.

Medicine

Abu Bakr Muhammad ibn Zakariyya' al-Razi, a Persian (d. 925), was described by the Orientalist Max Mayerhof, as 'the greatest physician of the Islamic period' and one of the greatest doctors of all time. He was the first person to diagnose measles and smallpox and to use the animal gut for sutures. Of the many works of al-Razi, probably the best known is his 24-volume encyclopaedia, 'The Comprehensive Book of Medicine' (*Kitab al-Hawifi't-Tibb*).

Abu 'Ali al-Husayn ibn Sina, better known in Europe as 'Avicenna', is probably the most significant philosopher and traveller to emerge from the Islamic world. His encyclopaedia on medicine, the 'Canon' (*al-Qanun fi'l-Tibb*) continued to be taught as a medical textbook in Europe until the seventeenth century.

Al-Hassan ibn al-Haytham (b. 965) is known to have been an excellent astronomer, physicist, mathematician and doctor. He was the first scholar to teach that light 'does not originate from the eye but enters the eye'. Until al-Haytham's thesis, the Greeks and Romans thought that the eye sent out visual rays to the objects it sees. Among other ideas, he discussed the propagation of light and colours, optical illusions and reflections. He also formulated experiments to test the angles of incidence and reflection.

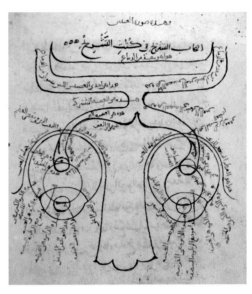

4.3 Al-Haytham's sketch of the human optic system

Botany

Ahmad ibn al-Baitar is a well-known botanist and pharmacist. He collected plants in and around Andalusia in Spain and along the North African coast. Ibn al-Baitar's best known work, *Kitab Al-Jame'*, described medicines and nutrients that could be derived from plants, animals, and minerals. His work was widely referred by botanists/pharmacists until the eighteenth century.

Mathematics

Abu Rayhan Muhammad ibn Ahmad al-Biruni (b. 973) is regarded as one of the greatest Islamic scholars and was well versed in physics, mathematics, astronomy, and natural sciences. In addition to explaining the problems of advanced trigonometry, he

4.4 A page from a book about drugs made from plants

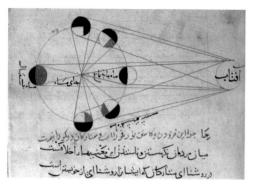

discovered that light travels faster than sound and accurately calculated lines of longitude and latitude on maps. Al-Biruni also discussed the rotation of the earth on its axis and his observational data is still used today in geophysics and astronomy.

4.5 Al-Biruni's illustration of the phases of the moon

Muhammad ibn Musa al-Khwarizmi (b. 780) was a mathematician, astronomer, astrologer and geographer. Best known as the inventor of algebra, al-Khwarizmi wrote the classical mathematical work *Hisab al-Jabr wa-al-Muqabala* (Calculation by Completion and Balancing), from which the word algebra was derived.

> **Muslim Culture**
> Muslims used decimal fractions at least 200 years before the Western world knew about them.

History

Abu Ja'far Muhammad ibn Jarir al-Tabari (d. 923) was a historian of such influence that the *Encyclopaedia Britannica* states that he 'laid the foundations for both Qur'anic and historical sciences'. Among his most famous works is *Tarikh al-Rusul wa al-Muluk* (History of the Prophets and Kings), a historical description of the Muslim world and the Middle East in 26 volumes.

Muhammad Ibn Battuta (b. 1304) is described as the father of exploration. He visited most of the Islamic world and many non-Muslim lands including Africa, the Middle East, India, Central Asia, Southeast Asia, and China. Frances Ward, in his book *Did Marco Polo Go to China?*, argued that Marco Polo never actually travelled to China and at best retraced the path of Muslim travellers, presenting them as his own.

Philosophy

Abu Hamid Muhammad ibn Muhammad al-Ghazali (d. 1111) was honoured with the title *Hujjat al-Islam* ('Proof of Islam'). His contribution to restoring the Islamic faith was so great, that it is said, if all of the books of Islam were destroyed and only Imam al-Ghazali's *Ihya Ulum Al-Din* ('Revival of the Religious Sciences') was preserved, this would be but a slight loss.

4.6 Golden Gate, where al-Ghazali wrote Ihya Ulum al-Din

Abu Yusuf Ya'qub ibn 'Ishaq as-Sabbah al-Kindi (d. 873) was a master polymath who was considered the 'father of Arab philosophy'. Al-Kindi wrote over 265 works, including 22 on philosophy, 11 on mathematics, 22 on numerals, 22 on medicine, 21 on politics, 33 on physics and 19 on astronomy.

CHAPTER 5

The Crusades
1095-1254

Under Muslim rule, Europe's Christians were allowed to visit holy sites in the Middle East, particularly Jerusalem. Returning European pilgrims brought with them stories of an advanced wealthy Islamic culture.

Al-Hakim, the sixth century Fatimid caliph, provided the perfect justification for a European invasion when he began to persecute not only Christians but also Muslim sects. His destruction of the Church of the Holy Sepulchre gave the ruthless Pope Urban II the pretext for an invasion. Urban called on Christians to take up arms and march against the 'Saracens' (a derogatory term for Arabs and Muslims), and to liberate Jerusalem from the 'infidels'.

With the Papal promise of heaven and, more importantly, the lure of great booty from the Muslim world, people in their thousands rallied to Urban's cry. Calls for holy war echoed across Europe. The Crusaders, as they were known, converged on Constantinople (Istanbul) en route to the Holy Land, persecuting and killing many along the way who disagreed with their mission, including fellow Christians.

> **The Crusades**
> The Crusades were a series of campaigns against the Muslim world, which began in 1095 and lasted until 1492.

The European forces joined the Byzantine army and advanced towards Jerusalem, capturing major cities along the way.

On Friday 15 July 1099, the Crusaders arrived at the gates of Jerusalem and lay siege to the city for six weeks, after which the city fell. Led by Tancred, Prince of Galilee, the Crusaders smashed their way into the Dome of the Rock mosque and stripped it of all its gold and silver. Surviving Muslims fled into the other great mosque of Al-Aqsa before surrendering. In return for safe passage they agreed to pay a ransom to Tancred, who proved untrustworthy. The next morning, the Crusaders re-entered Al-Aqsa mosque and slaughtered everyone. No one knows exactly how many were butchered but historians estimate that over 70,000 people died. One of the Crusaders spoke of struggling to walk through a knee-high mass of blood and bodies.

The Crusaders then turned their attention to the Jews. The Crusaders locked the Jews in their synagogues before burning the buildings, and all of their occupants, to the ground. Under Crusader rule, no Muslim or Jew was permitted to reside in the city of Jerusalem.

5.1 The statue of Godfrey of Bouillon in Brussels

Pope Urban's speech

Your brethren who live in the East are in urgent need of your help, and you must hasten to give them the aid which has often been promised them. For, as the most of you have heard, the Turks and Arabs have attacked them...On this account I, or rather the Lord, beseech you as Christ's heralds to publish this everywhere and to persuade all people of whatever rank, foot-soldiers and knights, poor and rich, to carry aid promptly to those Christians and to destroy that vile race from the lands of our friends. I say this to those who are present, it is meant also for those who are absent. Moreover, Christ commands it.

With what reproaches will the Lord overwhelm us if you do not aid those who, with us, professed the Christian religion! Let those who have been accustomed unjustly to wage private warfare against the faithful now go against the infidels and end with victory this war which should have been begun long ago. Let those who for a long time have been robbers now become knights. Let those who have been fighting against their brothers and relatives now fight in a proper way against the barbarians. Let those who have been serving as mercenaries for small pay now obtain eternal reward. Let those who have been wearing themselves out in both body and soul now work for a double honour. Behold! On this side will be the sorrowful and poor, on that, the rich; on this side, the enemies of the Lord, on that, His friends. Let those who go not put off the journey, but rent their lands and collect money for their expenses; and as soon as winter is over and spring comes, let them eagerly set out on the way with God as their guide.

(Fulcher of Chartres, Bongars, *Gesta Dei Per Francos*, 1, pp. 382 f., trans. in Thatcher and McNeal, *A Sourcebook for Mediaeval History*, pp. 513–517)

The Crusaders did not limit themselves to robbing every living Muslim in Jerusalem. After accumulating all visible treasures, they turned their greedy attention to the dead. Fulcher of Chartres wrote:

"

Our squires and footmen split open the bellies of those they had slain in order to extract from the intestine the gold coins which the Saracens had gulped down their loathsome throats while alive...With drawn sword our men ran through the city not sparing anyone, even those begging for mercy...They entered the houses of the citizens, seizing whatever they found...Whoever first entered a house, was to occupy and own the house or palace and whatever found in it as if it were entirely his own...In this way many poor Crusaders became wealthy. (Fulcher of Chartres, *Gesta Francorum Jerusalem Expugnantium* ['The Deeds of the Franks Who Attacked Jerusalem'], in Duncan and Krey, *Parallel Source Problems in Medieval History*, pp. 109–115)

"

The Dome of the Rock mosque was renamed Templum Domini and a cross was placed on top of the golden dome. Al-Aqsa mosque was renamed Templum Solomonis. Some Muslims saw the defeat as punishment for complacency and seeking a life of comfort. The way of Jihad had been forgotten and it was time to revive it. The Muslim sultan, Nur al-Din, began the process, and soon recaptured the cities of Aleppo and Edessa. This triggered the second Crusade.

Jews under the Crusaders

By the time the Crusaders were defeated, they had managed to decimate Palestine's Jewish population. In 1170, Benjamin of Tudela surveyed Palestine and found only 1,500 Jews.

The second Crusade (1147–1149)

The aim of the second Crusade, started in response to the retaking of Edessa in 1144 and Aleppo. It was led by King Louis VII of France and King Conrad III of Germany. Already defeated after attacks by Seljuk Turks on their journey to Palestine, the remnants of the two armies advanced towards Damascus, rather than recapture Aleppo which the Muslims had retaken. Harassed by attacks from Nur al-Din and the defending forces, the Crusader siege failed miserably and the French and German forces retreated.

Salahuddin

5.2 The statue of Salahuddin near the Umayyad mosque, Damascus

Salahuddin al-Ayubi was one of the greatest generals the world has ever seen. He was born in Iraq in 1138, and was brought up and educated in Damascus. In 1164, Sultan Nur al-Din sent his military commander, Shirkuh with his nephew, Salahuddin, to intervene in a dispute in Egypt. Their expedition was successful. Shirkuh was made vizier of Egypt in 1169, but died soon afterwards and Salahuddin succeeded him. When Nur al-Din died in 1174 he left behind his 11-year-old son as heir, who was manipulated by his none-too-faithful courtiers. Seeing this, Salahuddin returned to Damascus and took the reins of power.

In 1187, Salahuddin confronted the Crusaders, led by Reginald of Châtillon, at Hittin near Lake Tiberias in northern Palestine. The Crusaders suffered a crushing defeat and the road to Jerusalem lay open. Salahuddin, after a brief siege, entered the holy city peacefully on 2 October 1187. His generosity knew no bounds; he not only set all surviving Crusaders free, but also provided many of them with provisions for their journey home.

The Crusader's loss of Jerusalem led to a third Crusade.

The third Crusade (1189–1192)

The principal leaders of the third Crusade were King Richard I of England ('Richard the Lionheart'), the German Emperor Frederick I and King Philip II (Augustus) of France. The crusader leadership was in shambles. Frederick drowned on the journey. Philip and Richard were embroiled in infighting. Ultimately, Philip returned to France to plot against Richard.

Richard made several attempts to capture Jerusalem but was stopped by Salahuddin. Finally, on 2 September 1192 a peace treaty was signed. The treaty afforded the Crusaders control of the coast of Jaffa and Christian pilgrims were to have free access to the holy places. Within a month of the peace Richard left for Europe.

Five months later on 3 March 1193 Salahuddin passed away and the unity against the crusaders withered away. The new Ayyubid leadership entered into a truce with the Crusaders that provided the Europeans with a titular kingdom of Jerusalem, centring on Acre. This became known as the Second Kingdom.

European rulers, however, were not interested in pilgrimage, worship or partnership. They wanted total control over land and riches, and another Crusade was soon commenced.

The fourth Crusade (1202–1204)

Pope Innocent III, not giving up, roused the French by promising them Muslim riches as booty. The Crusaders made an agreement with the city of Venice for transportation to Egypt. When the Crusader army arrived in Venice, the fighting force was much smaller than anticipated and the accumulated wealth of the Crusaders was not enough to pay the agreed fee for the transportation. The Venetians, who had fulfilled their part of the bargain and provided a fleet of war galleys and transports, proposed that the Crusader army could pay its debt by helping to settle an old score as a down payment for the voyage. The Crusaders had no option but to help the Venetians and laid siege to Zara, a city in present day Croatia.

Once in Zara, the Crusaders met a refugee Greek prince called Alexius who told them that his father was the rightful heir of the Byzantine Empire. Alexius promised a handsome reward if the Crusaders helped his father regain the throne. The Crusader force accepted the offer and sailed for Constantinople. The Crusaders invaded Constantinople in 1203 and placed Alexius and his father Isaac on the Byzantine throne. By then, the Crusaders had accumulated enough wealth to satisfy themselves; foregoing the journey to Palestine, they returned home.

The Children's Crusade (1212)

One of the darkest episodes in European history is reflected in the Children's Crusade of 1212. European children between the ages of ten and eighteen, indoctrinated into believing that God would assist them since they were innocent and poor, gathered in their thousands to conquer Jerusalem.

30,000 children reached the shores of the Mediterranean Sea, having been promised that the sea would part before them allowing them to continue their Crusade. The children were vulnerable, and the sailors upon whom they now depended had ulterior motives. Once at sea, two of the ships capsized, drowning all of the children on board. Those who survived were sold into slavery and this ingloriously ended the infamous Children's Crusade. Even this tragedy was not enough to stop the Europeans, who had their eyes set on the glory of the Muslim world.

The fifth Crusade (1213–1221)

The fifth crusade was initially proposed by Pope Innocent III in 1213 as an attempt to retake Jerusalem. Following his death in 1216 it was left to Pope Innocent III's successor, Pope Honorius III, to organise the Crusader armies under the leadership of King Andrew II of Hungary and Leopold VI, Duke of Austria. A fleet of Venetian crusader ships left Split (now in Croatia) in 1217;

once in the Holy Land the forces came under the command of John of Brienne.

In 1217 Jerusalem was under Egyptian control. The Crusader's plan was to attack Egypt in order to force the rulers to surrender key areas of Palestine. In 1218, the Crusaders landed at Damietta, only to find themselves in battle against Malik al-Kamil, the son of the Sultan. Damietta resisted the Crusaders for a year and a half; in 1221 the Crusaders succeeded in taking the city. Buoyed with success, the Crusaders headed towards Cairo under the leadership of Pelagius of Albano.

This was a disastrous decision by Pelagius. The River Nile flooded ahead of them and a canal they had crossed flooded behind them. Trapped, the Crusaders attempted to retreat. Ultimately, in the face of continued harassment by al-Kamil's army and the loss of a great number of troops, the Crusaders were forced to surrender. The terms of surrender included returning control of the city of Damietta to the Sultan, and the Crusader army returned home empty-handed.

The sixth Crusade (1228–1229)

This was led by the Holy Roman Emperor, Frederick II, who had previously refused to take part in the disastrous fifth Crusade, much to the annoyance of Pope Honorius III. By the time he arrived in Acre, Frederick had been excommunicated and he was losing support from Christians. However, Frederick approached al-Malik and negotiated a treaty.

The treaty was signed in 1229 and Jerusalem, Bethlehem, and a corridor running to the sea were ceded. Exceptions were made for area of Al-Aqsa Sanctuary and Muslim of Jerusalem to be governed by separate Muslim administrators.

The Christians retained control of the city until 1244; in 1244 the Khwarazmian clans, whose empire had been destroyed by the Mongols (see below) laid siege to Jerusalem and razed it to the ground, leaving it in ruins.

The return of Jerusalem to Muslim control resulted in Europeans launching the seventh Crusade (1248–1254). The seventh Crusade was led by Louis IX of France, who aimed to invade Egypt and use it as a staging post to attack and retake Jerusalem. Once again, the Crusade was a disaster; Louis's troops were defeated by the Egyptian army, which was led by the Ayyubid Sultan Turanshah, and Louis was captured. Although Louis later made small gains, the struggle was largely futile. By 1291 the Muslims had retaken Acre, the last Crusader outpost in Palestine.

5.3 Reproduction of the Santa Maria, captained by Christopher Columbus

During the fourteenth and fifteenth centuries, numerous attempts were made to recapture Jerusalem, but they all failed. European interest in Jerusalem ended in 1492, when Christopher Columbus became the first European since the Vikings to 'discover' America. Over the course of the next few hundred years, Europeans colonised America and killed millions of Native Americans. The brutal European colonisation of America was a chilling episode that would be echoed disastrously by the Zionists in Palestine a few hundred years later.

CHAPTER 6

The Mongol Invasion
1255-1281

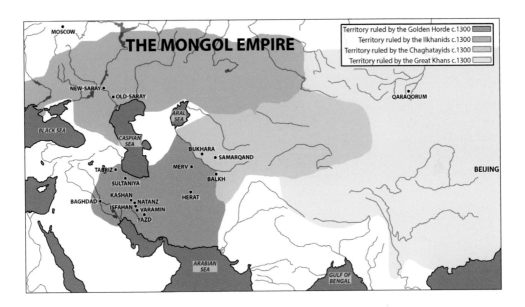

In 1196, Temujin, a Mongol who famously came to be known as Genghis Khan, began his campaign from the Asian plains. Khan crossed the Great Wall of China in 1214 and defeated the Manchus. After the surrender of Beijing, Khan razed it to the ground and turned west, conquering Turkistan, Samarkand, Afghanistan and Persia.

Khan died in 1227 at the height of his power and his successor continued with the conquest. The Mongols terrorised and conquered Korea in the east and sacked Moscow and Kiev in the west. They moved into Europe as far as Dalmatia and the Adriatic Sea, and conquered the Turks and Arabs in Asia Minor. In 1257 Kublai Khan (Genghis's grandson) came to power; by then the Mongol empire extended from the China Sea to the Mediterranean.

The Mongol threat forced the Muslims to enter into a treaty with the Crusaders, allowing them to govern Jerusalem whilst they focused on protecting the borders of the Islamic empire. The Muslim resistance could not hold back the Mongols and in 1258 they captured Baghdad. The Muslim Abbasid leaders were gathered together, wrapped in carpets and trampled to death by the conquerors' horses.

With the fall of Baghdad to the Mongols in 1258, the route was clear for the Mongol army to invade Syria and Palestine. However, the Mamluk forces in Egypt , who were now the custodian of Islamic power in the region, were able to check Mongol advance and by 1300 managed to push back the Mongols over the River Euphrates.

To Europe →

CHAPTER 7

The Jews in Europe
1200-1800

Jews were widely persecuted in Christian countries during the Middle Ages. Christians blamed Jews for Jesus's 'death', a concept known as 'blood libel'. This persecution caused Jews to practise their faith in secret and affected every sphere of Jewish life from the social, to the commercial and spiritual.

> o During the period of the Black Death in the fourteenth century, the massacre of Jews was common throughout Europe. Jews were accused of causing the plague by poisoning Christian wells.
>
> o Jews were despised throughout Europe; in many cities they were forced to live in designated areas and did not enjoy freedom of movement.
>
> o In 1215, the Fourth Lateran Council of the Roman Catholic Church, called by Pope Innocent III, proclaimed an official policy of restrictions and ordered all Jews to wear distinctive badges.

Spain

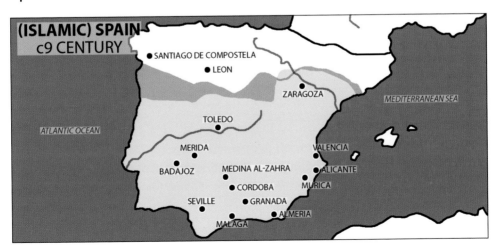

7.1 Gates of the Mosque of Cordoba

The Muslim conquest of Spain brought peace to the region and Muslim Spain became a safe haven for European Jews. Spain prospered and saw Jewish doctors, scholars and financiers rise to prominence. Following the disintegration of the Islamic caliphate, control of the Iberian Peninsula (Spain and Portugal) was lost to the Catholic 'Reconquista'. Once again Jews became third-class citizens; the view of Jews as the 'murderers of Christ' was often cited to justify their persecution.

In 1228, legislation was introduced to force Jews to wear distinctive badges; the incessant persecution of the Jewish people led many to convert to Christianity. Regrettably, this did not help Jews to avoid persecution; during the terror of the Spanish Inquisition which began in 1478, over 20,000 Jews were murdered and the remaining 160,000 expelled from Spain. Jewish expulsion from neighbouring Portugal followed in 1497.

England

Jews led a precarious existence in Europe during the Crusades; they were constantly harassed and lived in fear for their lives. Persecution of Jews in England led to a horrific event in York. In 1190, hundreds of Jews were gathered in a castle where they later committed mass suicide, rather than be massacred. Edward I (d. 1307) of England, confiscated Jewish wealth for his own benefit and expelled Jews in 1290.

7.2 York city gate

France

In 1394, the French followed the example of the English; King Charles VI passed an edict demanding the deportation of Jews from France.

> Most of the Jews expelled sought protection in tolerant Islamic countries and settled in countries like Turkey, Morocco, Egypt, and some, especially from Germany, settled in Poland.

Poland

The European hatred of Jews also emerged in Poland. During the persecutions of 1648–1658, numerous Jewish communities were destroyed by the followers of Bohdan Khmelnytsky, leader of the Cossacks in Ukraine. Jews were barred from craft guilds, farming and large commercial enterprises; they were forced to live by petty commerce, which led to a decline of Eastern European Jewry.

By the end of the sixteenth century, only remnants of old Jewish communities remained in Western Europe.

Summary

1100	*Germany:* 1,500 Jews flee.
1228	*Spain:* Jews forced to wear distinctive badges.
1266	*Poland:* Church decrees Jews cannot live with Christians.
1268	*Italy:* Jewish community totally destroyed.
1279	*Hungary:* Church decrees Jews must wear red cloth on their left side.
1321	*France:* 160 Jews buried in an enclosed pit.
1355	*Spain:* 12,000 Jews massacred by mobs.
1391	*Majorca:* 50,000 Jews killed.
1391	*Sicily:* Jews massacred.
1399	*Poland:* Renewed persecution of Jews.
1412	*Spain:* In Castile, Jews forced to live in separate quarters and wear badges.
1420	*France:* Jews expelled from Lyon.
1420	*France:* Jewish community of Toulouse annihilated.
1474	*Sicily:* Jews massacred.
1492	*Spain:* 160,000 Jews expelled, during which 20,000 die or are killed.
1492	*Sicily:* Jews expelled.
1492	*Malta:* Jews expelled.
1494	*Poland:* Jews restricted to certain area in Cracow—the first Polish ghetto.
1498	*Portugal:* All Jews expelled.
1541	*Italy:* All Jews expelled from Naples.
1550	*Italy:* All Jews expelled from Genoa.

Modern Europe

7.3 The Arc de Triomphe, Paris

Following the French Revolution in 1789, the development of Europe's nation states and the parallel rise of Protestantism in other parts of Europe, the situation for Jews in Europe began to improve. Legislation introduced in England by Oliver Cromwell in the middle of the seventeenth century, and in France by Napoleon in the late eighteenth centuries, encouraged Jews to return to Western Europe.

Still, intolerance and bigotry continued to grow in Eastern Europe, and Jews were institutionally persecuted throughout Russia and Poland. Jewish persecution worsened following the Russian occupation of eastern Poland (1772–1796); draconian restrictions across all facets of society were imposed on Jewish people. In addition to social exclusion, eastern European governments embarked on periodic massacres of Jews, known as 'pogroms'.

During the late nineteenth century the Russian Empire was struck by a series of economic crises. The recessions caused widespread misery and hardship, and resulted in a rebellion against the Czar. Conversely, instead of addressing the root causes of the rebellion, the Czar responded by scapegoating the Jewish communities in Russia and fanning the flames of anti-Jewish sentiment.

> **Jewish Migration**
> Around 2,366,941 Jews escaped the pogroms; only 55,000 settled in Palestine (i.e. 2.3 per cent).

Religious hatred was not the only cause of anti-Jewish hostility. In Russia, as in other parts of Europe, Jews were also envied because of their success as petty traders, estate agents, moneylenders and pawnbrokers. Peasants and officials viewed them as parasites, ruthlessly amassing wealth through profiteering and usury.

As a result of persecution and hostility between 1890 and the First World War (1914–1918), many Jews left Europe for countries such as Morocco and Turkey, and some went as far as South Africa, Canada, Argentina and the United States of America. Only a tiny minority emigrated to Palestine.

Back to the Middle East →

The Mamluks
1260-1517

The Mamluk Sultanate consisted of soldiers of slave origin. The Mamluks played a pivotal role in checking the Mongol advance into Syria, thus sparing Egypt and North Africa from destruction.

The first Mamluk prince, Malik al-Salih, drew his supporters mainly from Asia. One of the most famous Mamluk leaders was Baybar (1260–1277), who consolidated Mamluk power. On the military front, Baybar saw off Frankish remnants and lay the Mongol threat to rest.

One of Baybar's great achievements was the postal service; letters could arrive in Cairo from Damascus within four days of despatch. Besides the ordinary mail, a system of airmail using pigeons was also perfected.

8.1 The Mamluk Summer Pulpit, Al-Aqsa sanctuary

After the relatively tranquil reign of Baybar, one of the darkest periods of the Mamluk dynasty began under the Burji Mamluks. The Burji Mamluks began to oppress not only Jews, but Christians and even fellow Muslims; no one was spared from the heavy burden of taxes and political restrictions.

In the sixteenth century the Mamluks were defeated by the Ottomans in Syria and Egypt. From 1517, Mamluk territories reverted to the status of provinces within the Ottoman Empire.

In Arabic, slaves are referred to as Mamluk or in plural Mamalik.

8.2 The portico built by the Mamluks, Al-Aqsa sanctuary

CHAPTER 9

The Ottoman Empire
1517-1922

As the Mamluks ruled in the Middle East, Uthman (1299) laid the foundations of the Ottoman empire, with its capital in Bursa (Brusa), Anatolia. By 1366, the European and Asian lands bordering the new empire had been conquered and the fledgling state became more stable. In 1453 a new Ottoman leader, Sultan Mehmed II, defeated the Byzantines and captured the prized city of Constantinople (Istanbul).

As the Mamluk rulers became more tyrannical, their people turned to the liberal and compassionate Ottomans. North African countries were the first to be drawn into the empire; first Algeria, followed by Egypt and

9.1 Selimiye Mosque, Turkey, built in 1574

Tunisia. After the Mamluk's final defeat in 1517, the holy cities of Makkah, Madinah and Jerusalem were brought under Ottoman rule.

The Ottoman Empire expanded further under Sulayman the Magnificent (1520–1566), one of the greatest Ottoman rulers. Under Sulayman, the empire extended from Baghdad to Algeria and included Budapest and the Crimea. Sulayman is also credited to have built the magnificent walls encircling the Old City of Jerusalem, which survive today. Sulayman opened the cities of the Middle East to all, including Jews, who left European persecution for the safety of Ottoman lands.

By 1566, the Ottoman Empire had reached its peak of power and achievement, and was relatively calm for the next hundred years. This lasted until 1683, when the Ottomans failed in their second attempt to capture Vienna. This failure came to be seen as a watershed moment in the empire's history; the balance tipped and the empire slipped into a long period of decline. Incredibly, it was not until 1830 that the French invaded and annexed Ottoman Algeria. The Italians followed shortly afterwards and colonised Libya.

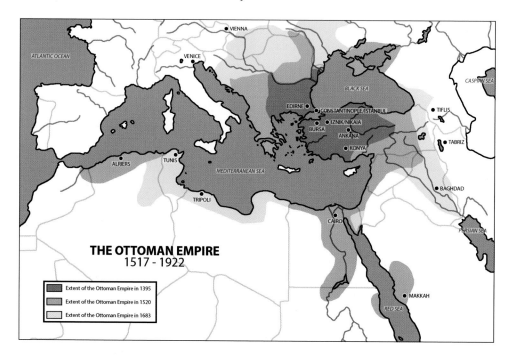

THE OTTOMAN EMPIRE
1517 - 1922

Extent of the Ottoman Empire in 1395
Extent of the Ottoman Empire in 1520
Extent of the Ottoman Empire in 1683

Throughout the Middle East, including Palestine, the Ottomans created the 'millet' system of governance, whereby each indigenous group was given limited autonomy with the Sultan in Istanbul holding the overall authority. With the benefit of hindsight, it appears that of all the laws passed by the Ottomans, one of the most devastating for the Palestinians was the Ottoman Land Code of 1858.

Ottoman Land Code
The Ottoman Land Code of 1858 allowed the government to declare uncultivated 'miri' and unregistered 'mawat' lands as state owned.

With cracks appearing within the Ottoman Empire, nationalism (a European import) spread throughout Ottoman lands. Ultimately, nationalism was one of the most significant contributing factor in the collapse of the Islamic Caliphate in 1922 and the subsequent redrawing of the Middle East map.

9.2 Part of the Walls of Jerusalem built by Sulayman the Magnificent

Summary

Until the beginning of the twentieth century, it is generally agreed that:

o   Jews suffered tremendously under the Christians and Europeans.
o   Jews found refuge under Muslim rule while Europe was persecuting them.
o   There was no conflict between Muslims and Jews.
o   The Holy Land was as peaceful as any other place on earth.

CHAPTER 10

The Seeds of Nationalism
1871-1908

Palestinian nationalism did not exist during the nineteenth century. However, in order to destabilise the Ottoman Empire Arabism, a precursor to Arab nationalism, was created (mainly by the British) among an Arab populace that was disgruntled by Ottoman rule. The European powers concluded that by encouraging Arabism they could occupy strategically placed Arab lands.

Schools based on the Western education model were the primary vehicles used to introduce nationalism in the Levant (Syria, Jordan, Lebanon and Palestine). In 1871, the Presbyterian Reverend Daniel Bliss, with the direct assistance of the US, opened the American University of Beirut. His ambition was that:

> **"**
>
> This College is for all conditions and classes of men without regard to colour, nationality, race or religion. A man, white, black, or yellow, Christian, Jew, Mohammedan, or Heathen, may enter and enjoy all the advantages of this institution...and go out believing in one God, in many gods, or in no God.
> (AUB, Digital Documentation Center)
>
> **"**

Missionaries brought an education system to the Levant that became the standard bearer of the region's elite. As more and more children from influential families passed through that educational system, a ruling class emerged that looked to the West for its solutions and standards. Much more crucial, however, was the system's ability to plant the seeds of nationalism.

10.1 The American University of Beirut

Aside from the influence of education, increased interaction between Arabs and Westerners played a major role in the new society. Political ideas were conveyed to the masses via the rapidly growing print media. The proliferation of publications was phenomenal, and by 1908 there were around 30 newspapers and magazines in Palestine alone.

Arab Nationalism

The first Arab nationalist party was formed by graduates of the American University of Beirut in 1875.

In 1876, Levantine Arabs forced Abdul Hamid II, the Ottoman Sultan, to draft the first constitution for ruling the Muslim lands. Abdul Hamid duly obliged, only to suspend the constitution two years later, which led Arab intellectuals to unite in rebellion. They formed the Committee of Union and Progress (CUP), now better known as the 'Young Turks', and in 1908 the Young Turk Revolution demanded the restoration of the constitution and attempted to depose Abdul Hamid.

The constitution was re-implemented, marking the first major victory for Arab Nationalism. For the first time people in Jerusalem, Baghdad, Damascus and other cities could elect their own representatives to an assembly in Istanbul. The Ottoman Empire was transformed from autocratic rule to consultative (or democratic) rule.

10.2 Wadi Rum, best known for its connection with British officer T.E. Lawrence

The Suez Canal

In 1858, the Universal Company of the Maritime Suez Canal was formed to build a canal in Egypt and operate it for 99 years, after which ownership was to return to the Egyptian government. The company was originally a private Egyptian affair, with its stock owned chiefly by French and Egyptian interests.

In 1875 the British government, which had initially attempted to block the digging of the canal, purchased Egypt's shares in the company. By 1915, Britain had over 100,000 soldiers stationed in Egypt to secure its economic interest in the canal.

10.3 Port Said waterfront

CHAPTER 11

Palestine at the Turn of the Nineteenth Century

Politics

Between 1887–1888, the Ottomans divided Palestine into three areas: Acre, Nablus and Jerusalem. A special status was accorded to Jerusalem and its immediate surroundings because it contained most of Palestine's holy sites, including Al-Aqsa mosque. Instead of being administered by the Pasha in Damascus, the Sultan made Jerusalem an autonomous unit linked directly to Istanbul, the capital of the Ottoman Empire. Abdul Hamid wanted to keep a close watch on increasing European interference in the internal affairs of the Ottoman empire and Jewish immigration to Palestine.

11.1 Nablus, nineteenth Century

In 1888, the total population of the three Palestinian districts was approximately 600,000; comprising around 60,000 Christians, 25,000 Jews and 500,000 Muslims. The authority of the administrative unit of Nablus extended over the areas of Tulkarm, Jenin, Tubas and Beisan. Acre's authority extended over Safad, Tiberias, Nazareth and Haifa. In response to requests from foreign Christian groups, Nazareth was brought under Jerusalem's control for a brief period.

Economy

Palestine's economy was reliant on tourism (mainly from pilgrims of the three monotheistic religions) and agriculture. Palestinian land was exceptionally fertile; and as the demand in world markets grew Palestinian produce became more accessible. Palestinian farmers benefitted immensely as cotton production exploded in the mid-1800s. Gaza supplied the West with grain and Jaffa became synonymous with citrus fruits and vegetables.

11.2 A flour mill, Nablus

Presses for sesame oil, tanneries and flourmills, as well as macaroni factories in both Jaffa and Jerusalem, were the backbone of the Palestinian economy. Stone, brick and ceramic industries were also drivers of the pre-First World War economy.

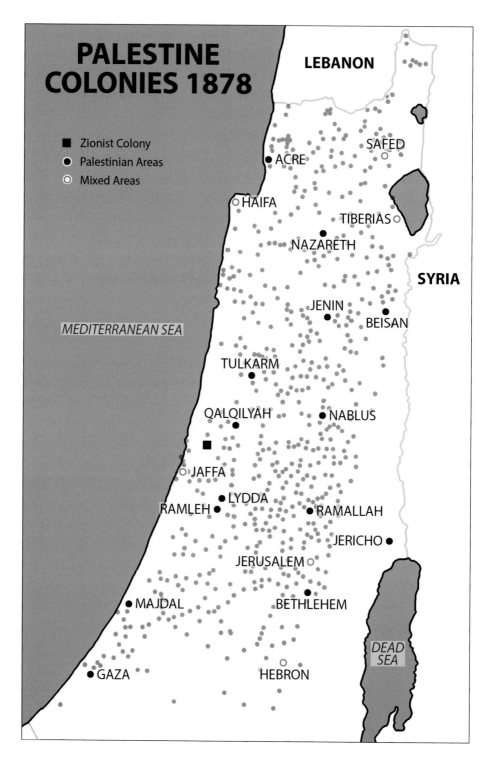

PALESTINE COLONIES 1878

LEBANON

■ Zionist Colony
● Palestinian Areas
○ Mixed Areas

SAFED ○

● ACRE

○ HAIFA

TIBERIAS ○

● NAZARETH

SYRIA

MEDITERRANEAN SEA

JENIN ●

● BEISAN

TULKARM ●

QALQILYAH ● ● NABLUS

■

○ JAFFA

● LYDDA

RAMLEH ● ● RAMALLAH

JERICHO ●

JERUSALEM ○

● MAJDAL

BETHLEHEM ●

DEAD SEA

● GAZA

HEBRON ○

11.3 A fruit seller at Damascus Gate, Jerusalem

The French bishop, Arculf, who visited the Holy Land towards the end of the seventh century, wrote about Jericho:

> **"**
>
> The whole site of the city is covered with cornfields and vineyards without any habitations. Between it and the Jordan are large groves of palm trees, interspersed with open spaces, in which are almost innumerable houses, inhabited by … men of the race of Canaan.
>
> (Wright, *Early Travels in Palestine*, p. 7)
>
> **"**

Meanwhile, back in Europe →

CHAPTER 12

Herzl and the Zionist Movement
1881-1904

The origins of the modern Zionist movement lie in the period immediately after the 1881–1884 pogroms of Jews in Russia and Romania. The first major pogrom took place in Elisavetgrad (now Kropyvnytskyi) on 15 April 1881. Jews continued to be attacked in Ukraine, Russia, Bessarabia, Minsk and Warsaw until the summer of 1884.

The emergence of the Zionist movement was in many ways a response to and a consequence of these pogroms. Though the movement did not have a unified leadership with a single aim, its social foundations were almost complete by 1884. Many groups, called Choveve Zion (Lovers of Zion), emerged in cities across Romania and Russia, inspired by the idea of 'auto-emancipation'. Auto-emancipation was an argument for Jewish self-rule and the development of a Jewish national consciousness, advocated by Leo Pinsker (1821–1891) and Moshe Lilienblum (1843–1910).

In the early 1880s, a small group of Choveve Zion members migrated to Palestine with the goal of rebuilding the ancient Jewish 'Kingdom of David and Solomon'. They used Zion as a symbol of hope and divine promise because the area where Solomon had built the Temple was referred to as Zion. The term Zion was previously used in reference to the fort that the Yebusite founders of Jerusalem built to protect the city. The Bible later referred to it as the citadel of David following his conquest.

As European pogroms spread, political parties emerged across Europe whose manifesto included the denial of social, political, educational and legal rights to Jews. European persecution of Jews in the late nineteenth century became known as 'anti-Semitism'; a term which emerged in 1879 through the pamphlets of the German agitator, Wilhelm Marr and his organisation known as the 'Antisemites League'.

This was the social backdrop into which Theodor Herzl, an Austrian Jewish journalist, was asked by his newspaper editor to report the trial of a Jewish army officer, Alfred Dreyfus, in France. The case illuminated the depth of anti-Semitism in the upper echelons of France's military and media, and its coverage had profound repercussions in elite Jewish circles.

12.1 Theodor Herzl

The Dreyfus court case changed Herzl, who came to despair for the plight of the Jews. Herzl felt that the only solution to anti-Semitism was either total assimilation with the Europeans or separation by establishing a Jewish state. In 1896, Herzl published his pamphlet *Der Judenstaat* (The Jewish State), and in effect became the founder of modern political Zionism.

Herzl worked towards establishing a Zionist state and sought the help of European governments to support his efforts. Aware of the intense rivalry between Britain, Germany and Russia for dominance of the Middle East, Herzl devised a plan to win the support of a major European colonial power. Britain wished to safeguard the sea route to India; whilst Russia sought access to the Mediterranean and Germany intended to build a railway linking Berlin to Baghdad.

Against this background of colonial rivalry, in 1896 Herzl wrote in *Der Judenstaat*:

> "
>
> We should there form a portion of a rampart of Europe against Asia,
> an outpost of civilization as opposed to barbarism.
> (Herzl, *The Jewish State*, p. 96)
>
> "

In relation to the local Palestinian population, he wrote:

> "
>
> We shall endeavour to encourage the poverty-stricken population
> to cross the border by securing work for it in the countries it passes
> through, while denying it work in our own country. The process of
> expropriation and displacement must be carried out prudently and
> discreetly...Let (the landowners) sell their land at exorbitant prices.
> We shall sell nothing back to them.
> (Herzl, quoted in Braun, 'A Basic History of Zionism')
>
> "

Basle: The First Zionist Congress

It was at the first Zionist Congress, convened in Basle in 1897, that Herzl proposed the creation of a state exclusively for Jews in any place possible.

> "
>
> If the Great Powers are prepared to grant the Jews as a people
> sovereignty over a neutral land, then the Society will enter into
> negotiations about the land which is to be selected. Two regions
> will be considered: Palestine and Argentina.
> (Herzl, *The Jews' State*, pp 147–148)
>
> "

12.2 Theodor Herzl at the first Zionist Congress in Basel in 1897

To Herzl's surprise, the most robust opposition he faced was from Eastern European Jews, who constituted the greatest majority of participants in the Congress (Orthodox Jews at that time completely rejected any Jewish political movement and did not attend the Congress). Although generally 'enlightened', Eastern European Jews would not accept any 'homeland' other than what they called the land of Zion, Palestine. Herzl wished to promote his new ideology and therefore accepted the 'land of Zion', i.e. the Palestinian, option.

Hence, the Zionist movement began with a small sub-section of Jews who felt that the problem of anti-Semitism could be solved by returning to their 'roots' and re-establishing the Jewish people in a land where their ancestors had once lived. The Basle Congress entrusted Herzl with the task of finding a colonial power to sponsor the Zionist project in Palestine.

The British author and playwright, Israel Zangwill (1864–1926) was one of Herzl's earliest and strongest supporters, although he eventually turned against the idea of establishing a Jewish state in Palestine. Ironically, it was Zangwill who coined the phrase:

> **66**
>
> A land without a people for a people without a land.
> (Zangwill, 'The Return to Palestine')
>
> **99**

This phrase became the potent rallying call for Zionist settlement in Palestine. It was not until 1904 that Zangwill realised that there was a fundamental problem with the Zionist programme. In a speech delivered in New York that year he explained:

> **66**
>
> There is...a difficulty from which the Zionist dares not avert his eyes, though he rarely likes to face it. Palestine proper has already its inhabitants. The pashalik of Jerusalem is already twice as thickly populated as the United States, having fifty-two souls to every square mile, and not 25 per cent of them Jews; so we must be prepared either to drive out by the sword the tribes in possession as our forefathers did, or to grapple with the problem of a large alien population, mostly Mohammedan...This is an infinitely graver difficulty than the stock anti-Zionist taunt that nobody would go to Palestine if we got it.
> (Zangwill, *The Voice of Jerusalem*, p. 92)
>
> **99**

Zangwill, and many other leading Zionists, split from the movement in 1905 when the Zionist organisation turned down the British offer to settle Jews in Uganda; a proposal which Herzl initially supported. The dissidents set up the 'Jewish Territorial Organisation' (JTO) to pursue alternative settlement proposals, with Zangwill elected as leader of the new body. After the Balfour Declaration of 1917, some of the JTO's leaders returned to the Zionist movement and it lost much of its influence. The JTO was dissolved in 1925.

> ### Jews against Zionism
> When Zionism first appeared on the world scene, most Jews opposed it and Herzl was only supported by a small minority. It was not until the full horror of the Holocaust was realised that the great bulk of the Jewish community came to support Zionism.
>
> (Goldmann, *The Jewish Paradox*, p. 77)

In response to Herzl's ideology, many Orthodox Rabbis openly condemned Herzl and Zionism. For religious Jews, the return to Palestine should only be brought about by divine intervention; human attempts to re-establish Israel are considered heretical.

Leading Jewish religious leaders who opposed Zionism included, amongst others: the Chief Rabbi of Vienna, Moritz Gudemann; the Chief Rabbi of Great Britain, Dr Hermann Adler; the Lubavitcher Rebbe, Rabbi Shulem ben Schneerson; the Holy Gerer Rebbe; the Sfas Emes; and the leader of the American Reform Movement, Rabbi Isaac Mayer Wise. These are notable personalities, but there were many more Jewish religious leaders who were also opposed to Zionism.

> ### Rabbis against Zionism
> In 1897, Rabbi Samson Raphael Hirsch, the religious leader of German Orthodox Jews, said it was a sin to promote Jewish emigration to Palestine. Rabbi Joseph Hayyim Sonnenfeld of Brisk called Zionists 'ruffians' and 'evil men'. In 1898, Rabbi Sonnenfeld wrote that Zionists had asserted views that the whole difference and distinction between Israel and The Nations lies in nationalism, blood and race, and that the faith and the religion are superfluous...Dr Herzl comes not from the Lord, but from the side of pollution.
>
> (Black, *Doten Sifte Yeshenim*)

Early encounters with the British

After failing to make headway with the Germans, Herzl turned to the British. At the turn of the twentieth century, a new round of economic crises in Russia had provoked renewed attacks against Jews; thousands sought refuge in England. The British public's attitude towards the Jewish immigrants was hostile and the influx of refugees was feared as a threat to Britishness. The British government, headed by Prime Minister Arthur James Balfour, set up a Royal Commission to investigate the issue of alien immigration.

In 1902, in response to pleas from Herzl's friends, the Commission agreed to hear him as a witness, despite strong opposition from Lord Lionel Rothschild, a leading Western financier of Jewish settlements in Palestine and an opponent of political Zionism. Herzl found a receptive ear among British politicians who were exceptionally keen to limit Jewish immigration into Britain, and to find a solution to what was referred to as the 'Jewish problem'. A common ground between Zionism and the aims of anti-Semitism were emerging at this early stage.

Whilst in London, Herzl stressed the need to help Jews establish their own national home. To support his case Herzl exploited the British fear of a Jewish revolutionary government. Herzl also presented the aims of Zionism as being at the service of British imperialism. He recognised that Britain, with its colonial interests in Asia, would be interested in the potential advantages Zionism could bring to the British colonialist agenda. Herzl was right. Joseph Chamberlain, well known for his anti-Semitic views and then serving as Colonial Secretary, showed an interest in the Zionist project. During exchanges between the two, a number of options for the Jewish state were considered: Cyprus, the Egyptian Sinai and Uganda. Given the fresh hostilities in Russia and the attacks in Kishinev during April 1903 when 49 Jews were killed, 500 wounded and thousands of homes and businesses looted, Herzl was now prepared to consider any of the three options as a stepping-stone to Palestine. For the salvation of the Jews he worked towards:

> **"**
>
> sovereignty ... over a portion of the globe large enough to
> satisfy the rightful requirements of a nation.
> (Herzl, *The Jewish State*, p. 93)
>
> **"**

Although Cyprus fell under the authority of the Colonial office, Chamberlain pointed out that his government was not prepared to evict its Greek and Muslim inhabitants for the sake of a new settler population. There were other problems concerning Egypt; constitutionally still part of the Ottoman Empire, it was not a British colony, though it had been under British military occupation since 1882. Ultimately, the British were not prepared to share Egypt with another Colonial enterprise and so the idea of a Jewish settlement in the Sinai was abandoned.

That notwithstanding, Chamberlain assured Herzl that Britain was prepared to place the Zionist project in one of its colonial possessions,

> **"**
>
> not inhabited by white settlers.
> (Bonds, *Our Roots Are Still Alive*, p. 26)
>
> **"**

On 23 April 1903, the Colonial Secretary proposed that Uganda, which then included present-day Kenya, would be an ideal location for the Jewish state. Although Herzl had previously committed himself to the settlement of Palestine, he was willing to consider other options. When the Sixth Zionist Congress was convened in Basle in August 1903, he argued passionately for the Uganda proposal. The suggestion was, however, defeated at the Congress due to strong opposition from Russian Jews, who demanded the Palestine option.

The Uganda proposal could have had disastrous consequences for the Zionist movement. It led to a split in its ranks and the emergence of the JTO under the leadership of Israel Zangwill, whose members believed that current circumstance, rather than historical attachment should be Zionism's guiding principle (see above).

Herzl approached many dignitaries from the Ottoman Empire advocating the case of Zionism. His actions led the Mayor of Jerusalem, Yusuf al-Khalidi, to write to Rabbi Zadoc Kahn of France in March 1899:

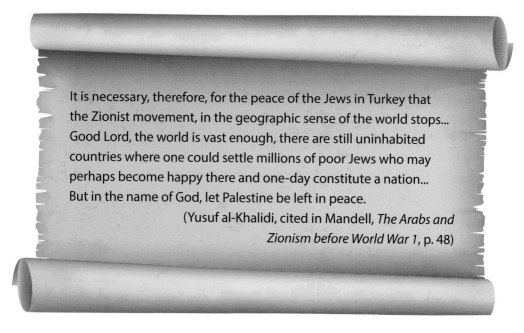

It is necessary, therefore, for the peace of the Jews in Turkey that the Zionist movement, in the geographic sense of the world stops... Good Lord, the world is vast enough, there are still uninhabited countries where one could settle millions of poor Jews who may perhaps become happy there and one-day constitute a nation... But in the name of God, let Palestine be left in peace.

(Yusuf al-Khalidi, cited in Mandell, *The Arabs and Zionism before World War 1*, p. 48)

The response to al-Khalidi's letter came from Herzl on 19 March 1899:

Let me tell you first of all that the feelings of friendship which you express for the Jewish people inspire in me the deepest appreciation. The Jews have been, are, and will be the best friends of Turkey since the day when Sultan Selim opened his Empire to the persecuted Jews of Spain …

The Zionist idea, of which I am the humble servant, has no hostile tendency towards the Ottoman Government, but quite the contrary this movement is concerned with opening up new resources for the Ottoman Empire. In allowing immigration to a number of Jews bringing their intelligence, their financial acumen and their means of enterprise to the country, no one can doubt that the well-being of the entire country would be the happy result. It is necessary to understand this, and make it known to everybody …

The question of the Holy Places?

But no one thinks of ever touching those. As I have said and written many times: These have lost forever the faculty of belonging exclusively to one faith, to one race or to one people. The Holy Places are and will remain holy for all the world, for the Moslems as for the Christians as for the Jews. The universal peace which all men of good will ardently hope for will have its symbol in a brotherly union in the Holy Places …

You see another difficulty, Excellency, in the existence of the non-Jewish population in Palestine. But who would think of sending them away? It is their well-being, their individual wealth which we will increase …

When one looks at the situation in this light, which is the true one, one must be the friend of Zionism when one is the Friend of Turkey …

And accept, Excellency, the assurance of my very high consideration.

(Theodor Herzl)

In 1901, Herzl attempted to entice Sultan Abdul Hamid with financial incentives and promises that included paying off all of the Ottoman Empire's debts, in exchange for Palestine. The Sultan, however, told Herzl:

> **"**
>
> I would prefer my body be dissected to small pieces
> rather than give Palestine away.
> (A. al-Naimi, *Al-Yahud wa al-Dawah al-Uthmaniyah*, p. 59)
>
> **"**

Herzl's Religious Beliefs

Herzl was not a religious man, and Zionism is a nationalist doctrine that has nothing to do with religion. Some quotes from his diaries:

… I do not abate a religious impulse … (Herzl, *Diaries*)

… I am an agnostic… (Herzl, *Diaries*)

I consider the Jewish question neither a social nor a religious one … It is a national question … Palestine is our unforgettable historical homeland … The very name would be a powerful rallying cry for our people.

(Herzl, *The Jewish State*)

Herzl wrote to Cecil Rhodes, the arch-colonialist who ran Southern Africa like his personal business and named a territory—Rhodesia—after himself:

> **"**
>
> Please send me a text saying you have examined my programme and approve it. You will ask yourself why I address myself to you, Mr Rhodes.
> It is because my programme is a colonial one.
> (Herzl, *Diaries*)
>
> **"**

Some early Zionists

Max Nordau, a French Zionist who visited Palestine, was so horrified to find that the region was well-populated that he angrily protested to Herzl:

> **66**
>
> But we are committing a grave injustice!
> (Wheatcroft, *The Controversy of Zion*, p. 84)
>
> **99**

Following Herzl's death in 1904, the Zionists continued to campaign for a Jewish homeland. When the nationalist 'Young Turks' overthrew Sultan Abdul Hamid II in 1909, the Zionists decided once more to raise the issue of settling Jews in Palestine. Herzl's successor, Chaim Weizmann, continued the search for a colonial backer for the Zionist project. With Weizmann's efforts a new phase in the history of the Middle East was about to begin, with Palestine as the Zionist's sole target for the new Jewish state.

CHAPTER 13

Britain: The Midwife
1904-1920

Weizmann's Progress

After Herzl's death in July 1904, Dr Chaim Weizmann, a Russian Zionist, became head of the World Zionist Organisation. Weizmann belonged to a wing of the Zionist movement that rejected the British government's offer to colonise Uganda. He recognised the need for an Imperial backer, but unlike Herzl he was not prepared to accept any offer. He had his heart set on Palestine and worked to exploit Britain's desire to have a foothold in the region. In 1904, Weizmann moved from Geneva to England; he was convinced that of all the European powers, Britain was the most likely to support the Zionist project.

Professor William H. Perkin gave Weizmann a letter of introduction for the position of Head of the Chemistry Department at Victoria University, Manchester (UMIST). Through Perkin, Weizmann was appointed as a lecturer in the department and became actively involved in the work of the Manchester Zionist Society.

> **Balfour in the British Parliament**
>
> ...a state of things could easily be imagined in which it would not be to the advantage of the civilisation of the country that there should be an immense body of persons who...however much they threw themselves into the national life...remained a people apart (Jews), and not merely held a religion different from the vast majority of their fellow countrymen, but only inter-married among themselves.
>
> (*Hansard*, 4th series, 1905, vol. 49, c. 155)

Though new to Britain, Weizmann quickly made inroads into the political establishment. This began in the winter of 1906, during the election campaign following the collapse of the Conservative government of which Arthur Balfour was Prime Minister. Balfour had heard of the Russian Jew who led the Zionist opposition against the Jews settling in Uganda, and the two met at the Manchester hotel that Balfour was using as his election headquarters. When asked why the Zionists were so bitterly opposed to the offer of Uganda, Weizmann said:

66

> Only a deep religious conviction keeps this movement alive.
> This conviction is based on the establishment of a Jewish state in
> Palestine, and in Palestine alone. If Moses had come into the Zionist
> meeting when it was voting for Uganda, he would have
> broken the tablets again.
> (Zagoren, *Chaim Weizmann*, p. 64)

99

The Conservative party was overwhelmingly defeated in the 1906 general election, though Balfour remained leader of the party until his resignation in 1911. From their first meeting in 1906, Weizmann cultivated a relationship with the former Prime Minister that was invaluable to the Zionist project. With the outbreak of the First World War in 1914, the time came for the Zionists to further their cause.

Ahad Ha'am, a prominent Zionist thinker and writer, wrote in 1891:

66

> What do our brothers do in the Land of Israel? ... They treat
> the Arabs with hatred and cruelty, unjustly trespassing into
> their lands, disgracefully beating them for no good
> reason and even bragging about it ...
> (Molisak, and Ronen, *The Trilingual Literature of Polish
> Jews from Different Perspectives*, p. 289)

99

Outbreak of the First World War

Turkey's entry into the First World War as a German ally had far-reaching consequences for Palestine. The Zionists took the opportunity to re-open negotiations with the British government for a Jewish 'national home' in Palestine. They emphasised Palestine's strategic geopolitical position and the importance of the Zionist population being willing to protect Britain's regional interests.

Following the collapse of the Asquith government and the appointment of David Lloyd George as Prime Minister in December 1916, British policy towards the Zionist project changed significantly. The government started official talks with the Zionists, who were ably assisted by C.P. Scott, the editor of the Manchester Guardian. Playing the role of facilitator, Scott introduced Weizmann to his close friend Lloyd George.

During the war, a strange turn of events worked in favour of the Zionists. Britain's ability to continue large-scale production of ammunition was seriously handicapped after it exhausted its supply of timber, which was used to produce wood alcohol from which acetone, an essential component in the manufacture of cordite, was made. When Prime Minister Lloyd George informed his trusted friend Scott that the government was looking for a resourceful scientist to invent synthetic acetone, the latter immediately recommended Weizmann.

Although a foreigner, Chaim Weizmann was employed by the British Ministry of Munitions and the Admiralty, where Arthur Balfour was now an influential figure. When they met, after Weizmann had taken his new position, Balfour assured Dr Weizmann:

> **"**
>
> I was thinking of that conversation of ours and I believe that when the guns stop firing you may get your Jerusalem.
> (Tuchman, *Bible and Sword*, p. 323)
>
> **"**

Realising the serious threat that German submarines posed to the Allies, Weizmann committed himself and Zionism to the British war effort with the understanding that Britain would reward them with a public declaration of support for political Zionism and its territorial aspirations in Palestine.

Why write to Rothschild?

In 1875, in order to raise funds the Egyptians offered shares in the Universal Company of the Maritime Suez Canal for sale, allowing the shareholder operational control. Although the French, Russians and Turks were all keen to acquire control of the waterway it was the British Prime Minister Benjamin Disraeli who was successful in raising £4 million to purchase the shares. This was achieved by obtaining a loan from his friend, Lionel de Rothschild. It was this friendship that led the British government to consider the Rothschilds as Jewish representatives for the Zionist movement.

13.1 The House of Commons, London

By 1917 Balfour was Foreign Secretary; his declaration was written a month
before the Ottoman surrendered Jerusalem in December 1917. Though consisting
of only 67 words, the 1917 'Balfour Declaration' is undoubtedly one of the most
decisive documents in the modern history of Palestine and the Middle East. It
became the cornerstone of the Zionist project, changing not only the region's
demographics but also its political, social and military configurations.

Balfour, the anti-Semite
Balfour … did not mind the Jews having a homeland of their own…
What he did not want was yet more Jews settling in Britain.
(Alderman, *Jewish Chronicle*, 31 May 2002)

The Balfour Declaration was a victory for the Zionist project, but a tragedy for the Palestinians. Acting as sole arbiter, Britain condemned the Palestinians in *absentia*. The process by which the Declaration was granted violated the legal maxim that 'no one can give that which he has not' (*nemo dat quod non habet*). This violation was and remains an injustice against Palestinians: how could one country promise the establishment of a national home for a second group of people in the homeland of a third, at a time when the first had no sovereign rights over the concerned territory?

Lord Balfour wrote in 1919:

> **"**
>
> For in Palestine we do not propose even…consulting the wishes of the present inhabitants of the country…(Zionism's) immediate needs and hopes for the future are much more important than the desires and prejudices of the 700,000 Arabs who presently inhabit Palestine.
> (Harris, *National Liberation*, p. 237)
>
> **"**

In June 1922 Britain attempted to clarify the Balfour Declaration. The resultant White Paper stated:

> **"**
>
> Nor have [the British government] at any time contemplated, as appears to be feared by the Arab delegation, the disappearance or the subordination of the Arab population, language or culture in Palestine…The terms of the (Balfour) Declaration…do not contemplate that Palestine as a whole should be converted into a Jewish National Home, but that such a Home should be founded in Palestine… (Moreover) the Zionist commission in Palestine…does not possess any share in the general administration of the country.
>
> **"**

Most members of the Cabinet were in favour of the Balfour Declaration, except Lord Edwin Samuel Montagu. Ironically, Lord Edwin was the only Jewish Minister in the Cabinet, and had written against Zionism in August 1917:

"

It is in this atmosphere that the Government proposes to endorse the formation of a new nation with a new home in Palestine. This nation will presumably be formed of Jewish Russians, Jewish Englishmen, Jewish Roumanians [sic], Jewish Bulgarians, and Jewish citizens of all nations—survivors or relations of those who have fought or laid down their lives for the different countries which I have mentioned, at a time when the three years that they have lived through have united their outlook and thought more closely than ever with the countries of which they are citizens.

Zionism has always seemed to me to be a mischievous political creed, untenable by any patriotic citizen of the United Kingdom. If a Jewish Englishman sets his eyes on The Mount of Olives and longs for the day when he will shake British soil from his shoes and go back to agricultural pursuits in Palestine, he has always seemed to me to have acknowledged aims inconsistent with British citizenship and to have admitted that he is unfit for a share in public life in Great Britain, or to be treated as an Englishman…it seems to be inconceivable that Zionism should be officially recognised by the British Government, and that Mr Balfour should be authorised to say that Palestine was to be reconstituted as the 'national home of the Jewish people'. I do not know what this involves, but I assume that it means that Mohammedans and Christians are to make way for the Jews and that the Jews should be put in all positions of preference…Perhaps also citizenship must be granted only as a result of a religious test.

"

66

I lay down with emphasis four principles:

1. I assert that there is not a Jewish nation…
2. When the Jews are told that Palestine is their national home…
    (they will drive out) its present inhabitants, taking all the best in the
    country…I have always understood, by the Jews before Zionism
    was invented, that to bring the Jews back to form a nation in the
    country from which they were dispersed would require Divine
    leadership.
3. …It is quite true that Palestine plays a large part in Jewish history,
    but so it does in modern Mohammedan history, and, after the time
    of the Jews, surely it plays a larger part than any other country in
    Christian history. The Temple may have been in Palestine, but so
    was the Sermon on the Mount and the Crucifixion. I would not
    deny to Jews in Palestine equal rights to colonisation with those
    who profess other religions, but a religious test of citizenship seems
    to me to be only admitted by those who take a bigoted and narrow
    view of one particular epoch of the history of Palestine…
4. …Why does Lord Rothschild attach so much importance to the
    difference between British and foreign Jews? All Jews will be
    foreign Jews, inhabitants of the great country of Palestine.

I would say to Lord Rothschild that the Government will be prepared to
do everything in their power to obtain for Jews in Palestine complete
liberty of settlement and life on an equality with the inhabitants of
that country who profess other religious beliefs. I would ask that the
Government should go no further.

(Lord Edwin Samuel Montagu, Public Record Office,
Cab. 24/24, 23 August 1917)

99

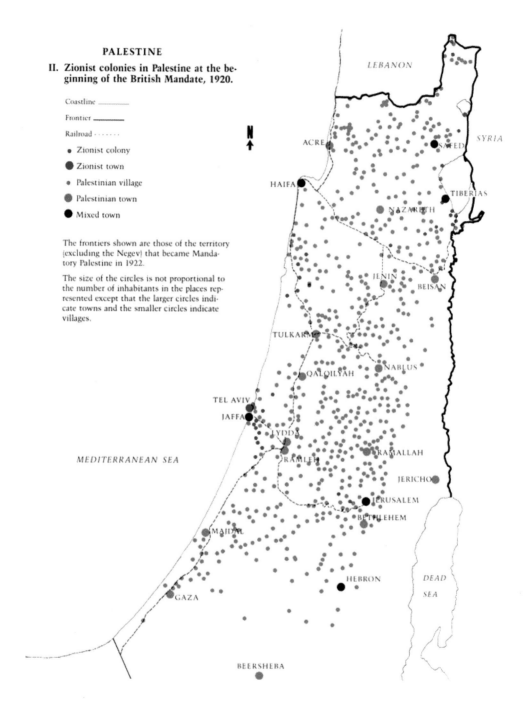

PALESTINE

II. Zionist colonies in Palestine at the beginning of the British Mandate, 1920.

Coastline ————

Frontier ————

Railroad · · · · · ·

- Zionist colony
- Zionist town
- Palestinian village
- Palestinian town
- Mixed town

The frontiers shown are those of the territory (excluding the Negev) that became Mandatory Palestine in 1922.

The size of the circles is not proportional to the number of inhabitants in the places represented except that the larger circles indicate towns and the smaller circles indicate villages.

LEBANON

SYRIA

ACRE

SAFED

HAIFA

TIBERIAS

NAZARETH

JENIN

BEISAN

TULKARM

QALQILYAH

NABLUS

TEL AVIV

JAFFA

LYDDA

RAMALLAH

RAMLEH

JERICHO

JERUSALEM

BETHLEHEM

MEDITERRANEAN SEA

MAIDAL

HEBRON

DEAD SEA

GAZA

BEERSHEBA

CHAPTER 14

The Middle East during the First World War
1914-1918

Britain found an opportunity to realise the ambitions of the Zionist project when the Ottomans allied with Germany during the First World War. Britain sought recruits for an insurrection against Istanbul and launched attacks on Ottoman interests.

Sharif Hussein of the Hijaz (modern-day western Saudi Arabia) was the first prominent Arab that the British recruited. Sir Henry McMahon was the British High Commissioner in Egypt at the time. McMahon approached Hussein, a

Hashemite Arab, for his support in exchange for the promise that independent Arab states would be created. Hussein to verify British policies wrote several letters seeking firm assurances that Britain would hand over the Hijaz to him and help create independent Arab states after the collapse of the Ottoman Empire. These letters, dated between 1915 and 1916, became known as the 'Hussein-McMahon Correspondence'. The correspondence assured Hussein that if the Arabs revolted against the Ottoman Turks, then the British would assist them and help to establish independent Arab governments. Some interpreted this to include an independent Palestinian state.

Abdul Aziz Ibn Saud (c. 1880–1953)

Grandson of Faisal, Sultan of Najd in central Arabia, in the early 1900s. Ibn Saud regained control of Najd, which had been lost by his father.

During the First World War, the British supported Ibn Saud's chief rival, Sharif Hussein. The proclamation of Hussein as King provoked Ibn Saud into invading the Hijaz in 1919. Hussein was forced to abdicate in 1924; his son and successor, Ali Ibn Hussein, was finally deposed in 1925. In the following year, Ibn Saud was proclaimed King of Hijaz and in 1927 he changed his title to the King of Hijaz, Najd and its Dependencies. In 1932 he renamed the land of Hijaz after his family and the kingdom became Saudi Arabia. Ibn Saud was king of Saudi Arabia from 1932 to 1953.

While the British were enticing the Arabs with nationalism and promises of self-rule, they signed agreements elsewhere that contradicted their promises to the Arabs:

1. In Europe the British allied with the French and signed the infamous Sykes-Picot Agreement. This agreement between the European countries shared Ottoman territories between the respective European powers.
2. To the Zionists they promised the creation of a Jewish homeland in Palestine.

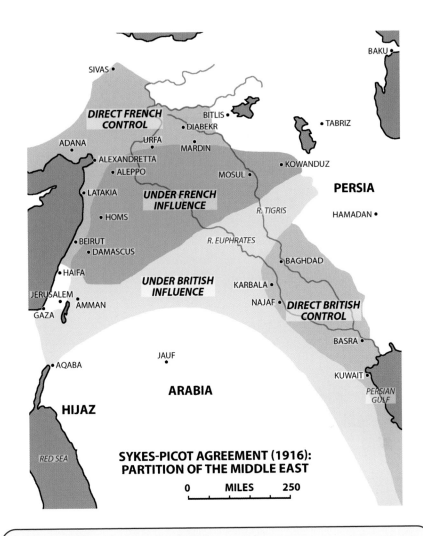

SYKES-PICOT AGREEMENT (1916):
PARTITION OF THE MIDDLE EAST

0   MILES   250

The Sykes-Picot Agreement

o   The Agreement was ratified in May 1916.
o   Britain would occupy Iraq, from Baghdad to the oil-rich Gulf and
     from Egypt to Eastern Palestine.
o   France would occupy Lebanon, Syria and southern Turkey.

The Allied forces, under the command of the British General Allenby, occupied
the whole of Palestine in September 1918. When Allenby entered the precincts
of Al-Aqsa sanctuary he boasted:

> **"**
>
> Today the Crusades have ended.
>
> (Armstrong, *The Spirit of Palestine*)
>
> **"**

When the First World War came to an end on 11 November 1918, the Arabs believed the British would reward them with a homeland of their own. The Zionists believed the same.

CHAPTER 15

Between the World Wars
1919-1939

The King–Crane Commission

Immediately after the First World War, skirmishes erupted between Palestinians and Jews. It became apparent that the aspirations of the French and British to rule over Palestine and Greater Syria could not be resolved with the will of the people. President Wilson of America set up the King–Crane Commission, comprising of Henry Churchill King and Charles R. Crane, to ascertain how the indigenous people of those regions wished to be governed. The Commission began its work in June 1919 and reported its findings on 20 August 1919.

The Palestinians, through intermediary and former mayor of Jerusalem, Arif Pasha Dajani, told King and Crane:

> **“**
>
> Zionism's triumph would mean Arab enslavement: "It is impossible for us to make an understanding with the Jews or even live with them…If the League of Nations will not listen to our appeal this country will become a river of blood".
> (Morris, *Righteous Victims*, p. 91)
>
> **”**

The findings and recommendations of the King–Crane Commission included:

o Ninety per cent of Palestine's inhabitants were non-Jewish and did not want a Jewish state in Palestine.

o A Jewish state in Palestine would violate Palestinian rights to self-determination.

o Zionists should find another place for their homeland.

Zionist leaders rejected the Report and responded by propagating an image of peace and friendship between themselves and the Palestinians. This public broadcast of affection, however, contradicted the private understanding of the Zionists as indicated by Ben-Gurion in a meeting held in 1919:

> **“**
>
> The conflict between the interests of the Jews and the interests of Palestinians cannot be resolved by sophisms. I don't know any Arabs who would agree to Palestine being ours - even if we learn Arabic…and I have no need to learn the Arabic language…On the other hand, I don't see why 'Mustafa' should learn Hebrew…There's a national question here. We want the country to be ours.
> The Arabs want the country to be theirs.
> (Segev, *One Palestine, Complete*, p. 116)
>
> **”**

The King–Crane Commission Report

The Commission recognised that the Allies had encouraged the Zionists through the Balfour Declaration. It also recognised that if the strict terms of the Declaration were to be adhered to, then the 'extreme Zionist Program' would have to be greatly modified. These strict terms included recognition of the statement within the Balfour Declaration that: 'that nothing shall be done which may prejudice the civil and religious rights of existing non-Jewish communities in Palestine' through the establishment of a national home for the Jewish people there. It further identified that a national home for the Jewish people is not equal to making Palestine a Jewish state and that the creation of a Jewish state cannot be possible without trespassing on the 'civil and religious rights of existing non-Jewish communities in Palestine'.

The Report also 'recommended…serious modification of the extreme Zionist program for Palestine of unlimited immigration of Jews, looking finally to making Palestine distinctly a Jewish state'.

Notes from the Report

o   No British officer, consulted by the Commissioners, believed that the Zionist program could be carried out except by force of arms.

o   That of itself is evidence of a strong sense of injustice of the Zionist program.

o   The fact came out repeatedly in the Commission's conference with Jewish representatives that the Zionists looked forward to a practically complete dispossession of the present non-Jewish inhabitants of Palestine.

o   The initial claim, often submitted by Zionist representatives that they have a "right" to Palestine based on an occupation of 2000 years ago, can hardly be seriously considered.

o   Jewish immigration should be definitely limited, and that the project for making Palestine distinctly a Jewish commonwealth should be given up.

After the end of the First World War the Allies (led by Britain, France and the US), held a conference known as the Versailles Peace Conference, to set peace terms for the defeated nations including Germany and the Ottoman Empire. As a result of the Peace Conference much of the Ottoman Empire was handed over to Britain and France as 'mandates'. The Peace Conference was also an opportunity for the Zionists to put forward their proposals for a Jewish homeland in Palestine.

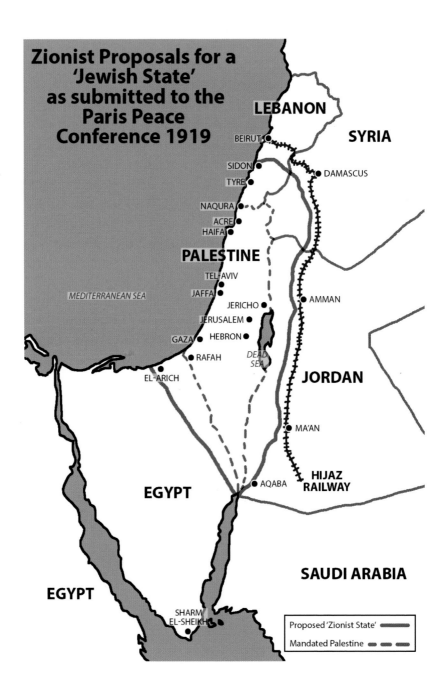

Zionist Proposals for a 'Jewish State' as submitted to the Paris Peace Conference 1919

LEBANON

SYRIA

BEIRUT

SIDON

TYRE

DAMASCUS

NAQURA

ACRE

HAIFA

PALESTINE

TEL-AVIV

MEDITERRANEAN SEA

JAFFA

JERICHO

AMMAN

JERUSALEM

GAZA

HEBRON

RAFAH

DEAD SEA

EL-ARICH

JORDAN

MA'AN

EGYPT

AQABA

HIJAZ RAILWAY

SAUDI ARABIA

EGYPT

SHARM EL-SHEIKH

| Proposed 'Zionist State' | |
| Mandated Palestine | |

However, not all Jews were in favour of the Zionists proposals:

> ### A statement to the Peace Conference by
> ### prominent American Jews
>
> Congressman Julius Kahn handed the following statement to President
> Wilson on behalf of prominent American Jews on 4 March 1919 for
> transmission to the Peace Conference at Paris:
>
> 'As a future form of government for Palestine will undoubtedly
> be considered by the approaching Peace Conference, we, the
> undersigned citizens of the United States, unite in this statement,
> setting forth our objections to the organization of a Jewish state in
> Palestine as proposed by the Zionist Societies in this country and
> Europe and to the segregation of the Jews as a nationalistic unit in
> any country. We feel that in so doing we are voicing the opinion of the
> majority of American Jews born in this country…
>
> Zionism arose as a result of the intolerable conditions under which
> Jews have been forced to live in Russia and Rumania. But it is evident
> that for the Jewish population of these countries, variously estimated
> at from [6–10 million], Palestine can become no homeland. Even with
> the improvement of the neglected condition of this country, its limited
> area can offer no solution. The Jewish question in Russia and Rumania
> can be settled only within those countries by the grant of full rights of
> citizenship to Jews …
>
> As to the future of Palestine, it is our fervent hope that what was once
> a "promised land" for the Jews may become a "land of promise" for all
> races and creeds … We do not wish to see Palestine, either now or at
> any time in the future, organized as a Jewish State'.
>
> (Tekiner, *Anti-Zionism: Analytical Reflections*)

In an address on 4 July 1918, President Wilson laid down the following principles
as one of the four great 'ends for which the associated peoples of the world were
fighting':

> **❝**
> The settlement of every question, whether of territory … or of political
> relationship upon the basis of the free acceptance of that settlement
> by the people immediately concerned, and not upon the basis of the
> material interest or advantage of any other nation or people which may
> desire a different settlement for their own exterior influence or mastery.
>
> If that principle is to rule, and so the wishes of Palestine's population
> are to be decisive as to what is to be done to Palestine, then it is
> to be remembered that the non-Jewish population of Palestine—
> nearly nine tenths of the whole—are emphatically against the entire
> Zionist program…To subject a people so minded to unlimited Jewish
> immigration, and to steady financial and social pressure to surrender
> the land, would be a gross violation of the principles just quoted, and
> of the peoples' rights, though it kept within the forms of the law.
> (David, *Arabs and Israel for Beginners*, p. 93)
>
> **❞**

Al-Buraq (Wailing) Wall incident, 1929

What the Jews call the Wailing Wall, or Western Wall, is part of the boundary wall of Al-Aqsa sanctuary. Jews believe that this is the sole remaining part of Sulayman's Temple. Muslims call this wall 'Al-Buraq Wall' after the Prophet Muhammad's 'celestial animal' that was tied to it on the night of Al-Isra (night journey) and Al-Miraj (Ascension).

In September 1928, groups of Jews placed chairs and screens in front of the Western Wall, arousing the suspicion of the Palestinians. This deliberate provocation violated the status quo that had existed between the cohabiting faithful from Ottoman times, and many Arabs believed a sinister plan was underway.

In August 1929, some 6,000 Jews marched through Tel Aviv chanting 'the Wall is ours'. Riots broke out first in Jerusalem and then throughout the country causing over 100 deaths on both sides, with around 339 Jews and 232 Palestinians wounded. The British authorities placed the blame with the Palestinians. They arrested over 860 people, 700 of them Palestinians; 25 were sentenced to death and three were hanged. All of the 160 arrested Jews were acquitted.

15.1 British police raid Palestinians at Damascus Gate

Following the 1929 clashes between Arabs and Jews over the Wall, an enquiry, the International Commission of Inquiry of 1930, was launched to clarify the religious status of the Wall. It concluded that:

> 66
>
> Al-Buraq Wall is part of the Al-Aqsa sanctuary compound.
>
> 99

The Commission also found that Al-Buraq Wall forms an integral part of Al-Aqsa area and is *waqf*, or a property under Islamic trust. Therefore, sole ownership and all proprietary rights to the wall belong to the Muslims.

In addition, the Commission found that the pavement in front of the Wall and the adjacent Maghrabi (Moroccan) Quarter (opposite the Wall) was also *waqf* property. The Commission ruled that Jews should have free access to Al-

Buraq wall for the purpose of devotions at all times, subject to the following stipulations:

> **"**
>
> The temporary instructions issued by the Palestine Administration at the end of September 1929, relative to 'appurtenances of worship' … are to be made permanent, subject however to one modification; it shall be permissible to place near the Wall the Cabinet or Ark containing the Scroll or Scrolls of the Law and the Table on which the Ark stands and the Table on which the Scroll is laid when being read from, but only on the following occasions:
>
> (a) At any special fast and assembly for public prayer that the Chief Rabbis of Jerusalem may order to be held in consequence of some public distress or calamity, provided due notice shall have been given by them to the Administration;
>
> (b) on New Year's Day and on the Day of Atonement, and on any other special 'holy days' that are recognised by the government as such days on which it has been customary for the Ark containing the Scrolls of the Law to be brought to the Wall.
>
> *Report by [HM Government] to the Council of the League of Nations on the Administration of Palestine and Trans-Jordan for the Year 1931*
>
> **"**

The Arab Revolt (1936–1939)

The Arab Revolt was based on practices of immigrating Jewish and exclusivity of land uses rather than Jewish population transfer and Zionist land purchase. However, these two factors made it possible to change the demography and political practices in Palestine.

The Jewish National Fund and Land

Established in 1901, the Jewish National Fund (JNF) was set up to raise funds for the purchase of land in Palestine for Zionist Jews. Once bought, the land was never to be sold back to Palestinians. Rich European and American Jews, in particular the Rothschilds, financed the JNF. From its inception the JNF enforced an apartheid system; only Jews were to cultivate the land they bought and Palestinians would not be employed.

> 1 dunum of land = 1,000 m² (square metres)
>
> 4 dunums = 1 acre
>
> A dunum was a unit of land area used in the Ottoman Empire. It represents the amount of land that can be ploughed in a day and is still in use in areas previously under Ottoman influence.

o   By 1914 Jews owned approximately 420,000 dunums.
o   By 1920 Jews owned approximately 650,000 dunums.
o   By 1943 Jews owned approximately 1,500,000 dunums.

This represents 5 per cent of the total area of Palestine.

> In 1943, Palestinians still owned 95 per cent of the land of Palestine.

Demography

Date	No. Of Arabs	No. Of Jews	Total population
1914 estimation	715,000	85,000	800,000
October 1922 Census	679,800	83,800	763,600
November 1931 Census	858,700	174,600	1,033,300
1940 estimation	1,078,600	460,100	1,538,700

The first half of the 1930s saw a dramatic increase in Jewish immigration to Palestine:

o   In 1929–1931, Jewish immigration was around 4,000 to 5,000 per year.
o   In 1932, the number was 9,500.
o   In 1933 the number rose to 30,000.
o   In 1934 the number rose further still, to 42,000.
o   In 1935 it increased exponentially to 62,000.

15.2 Jewish immigration to Palestine, 1930

By 1935 the Palestinians' patience was exhausted. The Zionists were not only taking over their land but had begun to practise apartheid-style policies by refusing to buy Palestinian produce, employ Palestinians or sell land to Palestinians. Concerned with Jewish political ambitions and the goals of the British administration of the Palestine Mandate, a group of Palestinians began a campaign of defiance. After a series of shootings between Palestinians and Jews, the Palestinians declared a general strike that lasted from April - October 1936. This was followed by a Palestinian revolt against the British administration.

The revolt lasted three years and cost the Palestinians dearly. Over 4,500 Palestinians were killed and nearly 6,000 were imprisoned. The most crucial loss over this period was the loss of Palestinian leaders who were either killed or fled to neighbouring countries. By the time the Second World War broke out, Palestinians were fragmented and exhausted from their struggle.

The Jews lost several hundred people during the revolt and suffered no significant loss to property. In fact, the Jewish immigrants consolidated as a unit and built three-dozen settlements during this period.

As a realist, David Ben Gurion recognised the nature of the 1936–1939 Palestinian revolt. In internal discussions he noted:

> **"**
>
> In our political argument abroad, we minimize Arab opposition to us…
> let us not ignore the truth among ourselves…politically we are the
> aggressors and they defend themselves…The country is theirs,
> because they inhabit it, whereas we want to come here and settle
> down, and in their view we want to take away from them
> their country, while we are still outside.
>
> (Chomsky, *The Fateful Triangle*, p. 91)
>
> **"**

15.3 British soldiers and Palestinian prisoners

The British Government White Paper (May 1939)

In order to pacify the Palestinians, following the Arab Revolt the British government published a White Paper that proposed the following:

o   Jewish immigration was to be limited to 75,000 for the next five years (until 1944).
o   After five years, all Jewish immigration will require Palestinian permission.
o   Jewish land purchase would be strictly prohibited in most districts.
o   An independent Palestinian state was to be created within 10 years (i.e. by 1949).

The British Commissioner, Thomas Reid, told a Jewish agency executive:

"

> Zionism was not a wise movement for the Jews to foster. It was the same nationalism that we objected to in Hitler.
> (Cohen, *Palestine, Retreat from the Mandate*)

"

Due to political weaknesses of the Palestinian society they failed to capitalise on the British offer; the influential Jewish community denounced the White Paper as illegal and said that it would never consent to British policy. Following this, the Zionists went on the offensive against the Palestinians and also the British. The right-wing Zionist militant group, Irgun, killed or wounded more than 80 Arabs in political violence; in Cairo in November 1944, Irgun murdered Lord Moyne, the British Minister of State in the Middle East.

> ### Haganah Terrorist Activities
> Haganah ('The Defence') was originally established by Jewish immigrants in the 1920s to protect Palestinian Jews against attacks. By 1940, Haganah was a Jewish paramilitary organisation that set up terrorist cells in Tel Aviv to produce mortar bombs, mines and grenades.

> ### Churchill on Lord Moyne's Murder
> If our dreams for Zionism are to end in the smoke of assassins' pistols and our labours for its future to produce a new set of gangsters worthy of Nazi Germany, many like myself will have to reconsider the position we have maintained so consistently and so long in the past. If there is to be any hope of a peaceful and successful future for Zionism, these wicked activities must cease, and those responsible for them must be destroyed root and branch.
>
> (Churchill, House of Commons, 17 November 1944)

Zionist Settlement Statistics, 1900–1939

o Between 1900 and 1939, Zionist colonies in Palestine increased from 22 to 200.

o From 1922 to 1939, Jewish land-holdings increased from 60,000 to 155,000 hectares (148,000 to 383,350 acres).

o From 1900 to 1939, the Jewish population in Palestine increased from 60,000 to 429,605, representing approximately 30 per cent of the total population.

The Zionists made no secret of their intentions for Palestine. As early as 1921, Dr David Eder, a member of the Zionist Commission, boldly told a court of inquiry:

> **"**
>
> There can be only one national home in Palestine, and that is a Jewish one, and no equality in the partnership between Jews and Arabs, but a Jewish preponderance as soon as the numbers of the race are sufficiently increased. He then asked that only Jews should be allowed to bear arms.
>
> (Hadawi, *Bitter Harvest*)
>
> **"**

CHAPTER 16

The Nazis and the Holocaust
1930 -1945

16.1 Nazi rally in Germany, early 1930s

During the Second World War, the Nazi German atrocities against the Jews, was one of the most barbaric. The Nazis murdered up to 6 million Jews in Europe as part of their 'Final Solution' to the so-called 'Jewish problem'.

Hitler's Abominations

o   1930: Hitler appointed Chancellor of Germany.

o   1935: Germany barred Jews from privileged occupations and German citizenship. It was made illegal for Jews to marry Germans and suspected Jews were investigated back to 1800 for 'Jewish blood' before a 'certificate of purity' was issued.

o   March 1938: Germany occupied Austria.

o   November 1939: 20,000 Jews taken to concentration camps. Jewish businesses, homes and synagogues destroyed.

16.2 Nazi Concentration Camp

Anti-Semitism in England

The way stateless Jews from Germany are pouring in from every port of this country (England) is becoming an outrage.

('German Jews pouring into this country', *Daily Mail*, 20 August 1938)

After Germany's occupation of Austria, America invited 31 countries to a conference in France, partly to discuss how to help Jewish refugees escaping German oppression. The Zionists boycotted the event.

> "
> The World Zionist Organisation refused to participate, fearing
> that resettlement of Jews in other states would reduce the
> number available for Palestine.
>
> (Quigley, *Palestine and Israel: A Challenge to Justice*, p. 26)
>
> "

Conference Resolutions:
o The US was to accept 153,774 Jewish immigrants (though only 23,068 were actually allowed to enter).
o France, which already had 200,000 Jewish refugees, asked others to share the burden.
o Argentina refused to take any more than the US, which was 23,000.
o The Benelux countries claimed to be full and could take no more Jewish immigrants.
o Although sympathetic, Britain escaped by offering sympathy, but little else.

The Zionist response to the Nazi threat

It was summed up in the meeting (of the Jewish agency's executive on June 26, 1938) that the Zionist thing to do "is belittle the (Evian) conference as far as possible and to cause it to decide nothing ... We are particularly worried that it would move Jewish organisations to collect large sums of money for aid to Jewish refugees, and these collections could interfere with our collection efforts..."

Ben-Gurion's statement at the same meeting: "No rationalisation can turn the conference from harmful to a useful one. What can and should be done is to limit the damage as far as possible".

(Evron, *Jewish State or Israeli Nation?*, p. 260)

American sympathy for the oppressed Jews of Germany

o   In 1939 the German ocean liner St Louis left Germany with 930 Jews on board, most of them with valid visas to the US. When the ship docked in Cuba on route to Miami, immigration officers refused the Jews entry, as their entry number had not yet come up. The ship was not allowed to dock in Miami and returned to Belgium.

o   In 1940, Congress decided not to allow 20,000 Jewish children into the US.

o   In 1941, the US passed new immigration laws that made it impossible for persecuted German Jews to enter the US.

> **What signal was America sending to Hitler?**

In light of the influence and affluence of many Zionists, why did the Western world turn its back on the suffering of the Jews under the Nazis and closed their borders?

> 66
>
> If I knew it would be possible to save all the (Jewish) children in Germany by bringing them to England, and only half of them by transporting them to *Eretz Israel* (Palestine), then I would opt for the second alternative. For we must weigh not only the life of these children but also the history of the people of Israel.
>
> (Ben-Gurion, December 1938, quoted in Davis, *Apartheid Israel*, p. 16)
>
> 99

Ben-Gurion worried that 'human conscience' might convince various countries to open their doors to Jewish refugees from Germany.

> 66
>
> He saw this as a threat [to the construction of a Jewish Homeland in Palestine] and warned: 'Zionism is in danger'.
>
> (Segev, *The Seventh Million*, p. 28)
>
> 99

This attitude demonstrates the Zionist leadership's priority to establish a Zionist state in Palestine, even at the expense of saving Jews from Nazism. An example of this prioritisation can be seen in the Zionists' sabotage of Rafael Trujillo (dictator of the Dominican Republic)'s offer to absorb 100,000 refugees and other similar proposals to settle Jews in Alaska and the Philippines.

> **Polish Jews against Zionism**
>
> In 1936 the Jewish political party, the Social Democratic Bund, won a sweeping victory in the Jewish Kehilla elections in Poland. The party's key policies included 'an unyielding hostility to Zionism' and to the Zionist enterprise of Jewish emigration from Poland to Palestine. The Bund wanted Polish Jews to fight anti-Semitism in Poland by remaining there. The Zionist goal was also opposed as a matter of principle by all major parties and movements amongst pre-1939 Polish Jewry.

❝

The catastrophe of European Jewry is not, in a direct manner, my business … [Ben Gurion] said in December 1942 … In the words of Yitzhak Gruenbaum … "Zionism is above everything".
(Morris, *Righteous Victims*, p. 162)

❞

After the Second World War, American soldiers in Germany presided over camps full of Jewish displaced persons (DPs) waiting for the chance to resettle in America, Europe, or the Middle East. The organisation that officially helped the DPs emigrate was the Jewish Agency, but after some time the paramilitary group Irgun (then led by Menachem Begin) and Lehi, an offshoot of Irgun also known as the 'Stern Gang' (led by Yitzak Shamir) began 'recruiting' in the DP camps.

66

[In 1947] the U.N. appointed a special body, The United Nations
Special Committee on Palestine (UNSCOP), to make the decision over
Palestine and UNSCOP members were asked to visit the camps of
Holocaust survivors. Many of these survivors wanted to emigrate to the
United States, a wish that undermined the Zionist claim that the fate
of European Jewry was connected to that of the Jewish community
in Palestine. When UNSCOP representatives arrived at the camps,
they were unaware that backstage manipulations were limiting their
contacts solely to survivors who wished to emigrate to Palestine.

(Pappé, *The Link*, March 1998)

99

Report of the Office of the Military Government
for Germany, January 10th, 1948

Tensions and clashes in the Jewish DP camps are now on the increase.
They are spreading to various parts of the US zone and are gaining
momentum. In the back of it all is an attempt and determination of
the Irgun Zvai Lumi to gain control of the camp administrations and
institutions.

They find it hard however to take over committees that are
democratically elected and are working under an army charter and
subject to public control and scrutiny. Irgun, therefore, seems to
concentrate on the DP police force. This is an old technique in Eastern
Europe and in all police states. By controlling the police, a small,
unscrupulous group of determined people can impose its will on a
peaceful and inarticulate majority, it is done by threats, intimidation,
by violence and if need be by bloodshed … They have embarked upon
a course of violence within the camps.

(Cited in Green, *Taking Sides*, p. 49)

President Roosevelt's adviser explained why Jewish refugees were not offered asylum in the United States after the Second World War:

> **"**
>
> What if Canada, Australia, South America, England and the United States were all to open a door to some migration? Even today [written in 1947] it is my judgement, and I have been in Germany since the war, that only a minority of the Jewish DPs [displaced persons] would choose Palestine …
>
> [Roosevelt] proposed a world budget for the easy migration of the 500,000 beaten people of Europe. Each nation should open its doors for some thousands of refugees…So he suggested that during my trips for him to England during the war I sound out in a general, unofficial manner the leaders of British public opinion, in and out of the government…The simple answer: Great Britain will match the United States, man for man, in admissions from Europe.
>
> It seemed all settled. With the rest of the world probably ready to give haven to 200,000, there was a sound reason for the President to press Congress to take in at least 150,000 immigrants after the war… It would free us from the hypocrisy of closing our doors while making sanctimonious demands on the Arabs…But it did not work out…
>
> The failure of the leading Jewish organisations to support with zeal this immigration program may have caused the President not to push forward with it at that time…I talked to many people active in Jewish organisations. I suggested the plan…I was amazed and even felt insulted when active Jewish leaders decried, sneered, and then attacked me as if I were a traitor…
>
> I think I know the reason for much of the opposition. There is a deep, genuine, often fanatical emotional vested interest in putting over the Palestinian movement (Zionism). Men like Ben Hecht are little concerned about human blood if it is not their own.
>
> (Ernst, *So Far, So Good*)
>
> **"**

CHAPTER 17

The British Mandate and the United Nations
1939-1949

Palestine during the Second World War

After the war was declared on 3 September 1939, the Jews and Arabs in Palestine allied themselves with the British. On 8 September 1939, Ben-Gurion told leaders of the Haganah, a Zionist paramilitary group operating in British Mandated Palestine:

> **"**
>
> The First World War ... had given us the Balfour Declaration.
> This time we must bring about a Jewish state.
> (Morris, *Righteous Victims*, p. 168)
>
> **"**

The Zionists convinced Britain to raise a Jewish Battalion as part of the British army, which was created in 1940. By September 1944, Churchill had further appeased the Zionists and ordered the establishment of a Jewish Brigade under its own blue-and-white flag. This was trained to high military standards and saw action in Italy.

By 1942, Britain's military intelligence service, MI6, estimated that Haganah had 30,000 members with sufficient weapons to arm approximately 70 per cent of them. The Irgun terror group had over 1,000 highly trained

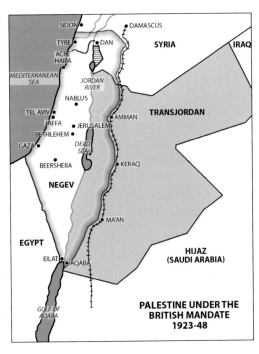

PALESTINE UNDER THE
BRITISH MANDATE
1923-48

men, with several thousand supporters. By 1944, Haganah had increased its size to 36,000 active members.

The Zionists capitalised on their war efforts; they not only acquired arms from the British but also procured specialist training. In mid-1941 Haganah, with Britain's aid, established the Palmach, a commando unit and strike force. By 1945, this highly specialised unit had 2,000 members and a further 32,000 Jewish soldiers, trained by the British Army.

In October 1941, Churchill wrote in a secret Cabinet minute:

> **"**
>
> I may say at once that if Britain and the United States emerge victorious from the war, the creation of a great Jewish state in Palestine inhabited [sic] by millions of Jews will be one of the leading features of the Peace Conference discussions.
>
> (Zweig, *Britain and Palestine during the Second World War*, p. 112)
>
> **"**

The Zionists soon began attacking British interests, a campaign that started well before the end of the war on 1 February 1944. As well as the assassination of Lord Moyne (see above), the Zionists blew up and attacked government buildings in Palestine, including police stations. They also attempted to assassinate the British High Commissioner, Sir Harold McMichael, on 8 August 1944.

Zionist terrorism

Extremist Zionist activities escalated soon after the war:
o   In May 1945: Zionists blew up telegraph poles, police stations and petroleum pipelines.
o   In July 1945: Zionists blew up a bridge near Yavneh.
o   In October 1945: a British detention camp was attacked and 208 illegal Jewish immigrants were helped to escape.
o   November 1945: The atrocities worsened as Zionists attacked and sabotaged railway tracks at 153 different locations around Palestine.

o   In June 1946: Zionist terrorist activities reached a critical stage when they
    blew up 11 bridges in one day, severing connections between Palestine and
    Trans-Jordan, Syria, Lebanon and the Sinai.
o   On 22 July 1946: the Zionist paramilitary groups Irgun and the Stern Gang
    blew up the King David Hotel in Jerusalem, killing 92 and injuring 58.
o   1 March 1947: Zionist terrorists killed more than 20 British servicemen.
o   13 March 1947: Zionist terrorists sabotaged the Haifa oil refinery; it took
    three weeks to extinguish the fire.

17.1 King David Hotel, Jerusalem   *17.2 The King David Hotel after the Zionist bombing*

The Zionist's terrorist activities against an increasingly frustrated UK culminated
in April 1947, when the UK asked the fledgling United Nations (UN) to consider
the future of Palestine. This did not deter Zionist terrorists, and if anything
emboldened them to intensify their campaign against Britain:

o   4 May 1947: Zionist extremists stormed the British prison at Acre and set
    criminals free.
o   12 July 1947: Zionist terrorists abducted and hanged two British sergeants,
    Clifford Martin and Mervyn Paice. Their bodies were booby-trapped, and
    when a British captain went to cut the bodies down he was seriously injured.

In August 1947, Britain announced that it would evacuate Palestine on 13
November of that year.

17.3 British Sergeants, Martin and Paice were hanged by Zionist terrorists

The UN Partition plan: November 1947

Even before Britain had decided to abandon its mandate, the Zionists had started to lobby President Truman of America and other world leaders for the establishment of a Jewish state in Palestine.

Under the direct influence of the US, the United Nations put forward a plan for partition, and after much lobbying by the US, a vote was held on 29 November 1947. The resolution to partition Palestine required a two-thirds majority to be successful. Of the 56 countries voting, 33 voted yes, 13 said no and 10 abstained.

> **UN Voting Results**
> The UN resolution to partition was passed by only three votes of the two-thirds majority needed.

The resolution proposed that the Jews be given 55 per cent of the land of Palestine, even though at the time of the vote they only constituted 37 per cent of the population (678,000 Jews, 1,269,000 Palestinians) and owned 7 per cent of the land.

The Palestinians, understandably, pressed the UN as to why it was not possible for the Jews to live as a minority in a single Palestinian state; and resisted the UN's decision that it was fair to turn almost half of Palestine's indigenous population into a minority under alien Israeli rule. The Arabs objected and asked for an international court to intervene and decide whether the UN could partition a country against the will and consent of its people; the Arabs were ignored.

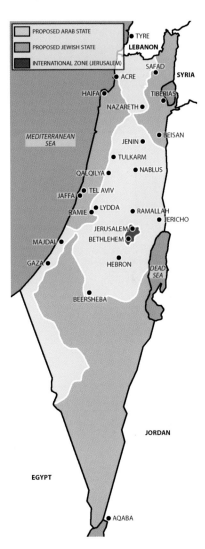

The US changes its mind

- o In early March 1948, the US realised the folly and undemocratic nature of forcing partition on the Palestinian people and went on record to oppose the forced partition of Palestine.
- o On 19 March 1948, the US called for the suspension of UN efforts to partition Palestine.

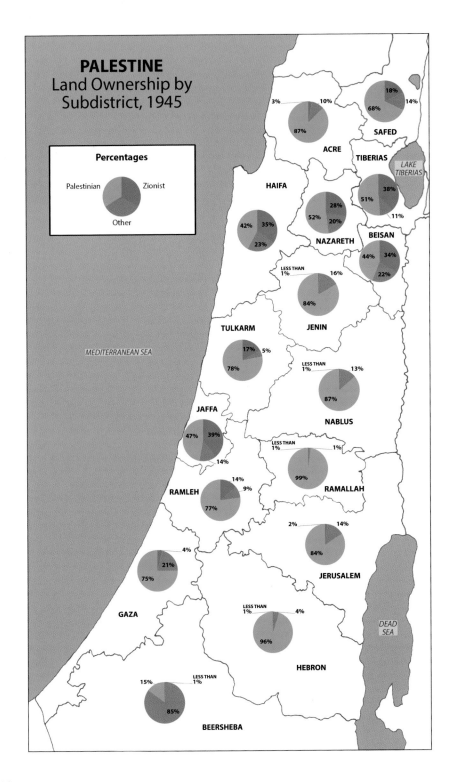

PALESTINE
Land Ownership by
Subdistrict, 1945

Percentages

Palestinian — Zionist

Other

ACRE
3% · 10% · 87%

SAFED
18% · 14% · 68%

TIBERIAS
38% · 11% · 51%

HAIFA
42% · 35% · 23%

NAZARETH
52% · 28% · 20%

BEISAN
44% · 34% · 22%

JENIN
LESS THAN 1% · 16% · 84%

TULKARM
17% · 5% · 78%

NABLUS
LESS THAN 1% · 13% · 87%

MEDITERRANEAN SEA

JAFFA
47% · 39% · 14%

RAMALLAH
LESS THAN 1% · 1% · 99%

RAMLEH
14% · 9% · 77%

JERUSALEM
2% · 14% · 84%

GAZA
4% · 21% · 75%

HEBRON
LESS THAN 1% · 4% · 96%

LAKE TIBERIAS

DEAD SEA

BEERSHEBA
15% · LESS THAN 1% · 85%

Statement by the Committee of the Christian Union of Palestine, 3 March 1948:

> **"**
>
> The Christian Union wishes to declare, in unequivocal terms, that it
> denounces the partition plan, being of the strong conviction that this
> plan involves a violation of the sacredness of the Holy Land which, by
> its nature and history, is indivisible, and represents an encroachment
> on the natural rights of the Arabs, the people of the country.
> (Nakhleh, *Encyclopaedia of the Palestine Problem*)
>
> **"**

CHAPTER 18

Zionist Aggression
1947-1949

As soon as the UN Resolution for the partition of Palestine was passed, trouble erupted once again in Palestine. The Zionists were well prepared for military action, while the Palestinians reacted to the injustice through public demonstrations.

The Zionists' portrayal of the trouble presented themselves as victims of another oppressive majority; that they were only 650,000 Jews surrounded by over 1 million ruthless Palestinians, and that God gave them victory. This portrayal is at odds with the reality of the situation.

Benny Morris, a Zionist historian at Ben-Gurion University, observed in *Righteous Victims* that the Jews, population and numbers aside:

> **"**
>
> ...enjoyed advantage over the Arabs in all other indices of strength -
> 'national' organization for war, trained manpower, weaponry,
> weapons production, morale and motivation and above
> all command and control.
>
> **"**

By the end of November 1947, the Zionists were armed and ready. By this time they possessed:

o   16,000 light weapons.
o   1,000 machine guns.
o   750 light mortars.
o   Trench works, bunkers and bomb shelters with barbed wire permit fences and minefields in 300 Jewish villages.

The Zionists were less like a powerless minority, and more like an armed and organised militia.

The Deir Yassin massacre (9–10 April 1948)

18.1 Present dwellings at Deir Yassin

Of all the massacres in the history of Palestine, the most infamous was carried out by Zionist terrorists at the village of Deir Yassin.

This massacre became a symbol of Zionist aggression against the Palestinians, as well as an example of Zionist treachery. The village mukhtar (head) had agreed with the Zionists to provide information on the movement of strangers in the area

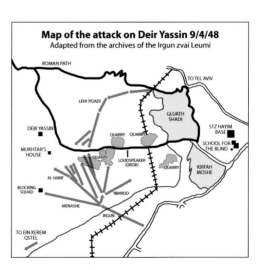

Map of the attack on Deir Yassin 9/4/48
Adapted from the archives of the Irgun zvai Leumi

ROMAN PATH

TO TEL AVIV

LEHI (YOAD)

GLUATH
SHADI

DEIR YASSIN

STZ HAYIM
BASE

QUARRY   QUARRY

SCHOOL FOR
THE BLIND

MUKHTAR'S
HOUSE

QUARRY

LOUDSPEAKER
(DROR)

QUARRY

KIRFAH
MOSHE

M. HARIF

BLOCKING
SQUAD

NIMROD

MENASHE

IRGUN

TO EIN KEREM
QSTEL

and other intelligence, on condition that the village would be left in peace.

The Zionists did not keep their word. At 4:30 am on Friday 9 April 1948, members of the Irgun, a Zionist terrorist gang, surrounded Deir Yassin and embarked on an orgy of killing and looting that lasted two days. Men, women and children were butchered and women raped.

18.2 The ruins of Deir Yassin

A chilling account of the massacre was given by a Red Cross doctor who witnessed what one of the terrorists called 'the mopping up' of the village; as Irgun militia attacked villagers with machine guns and grenades and finished off victims with knives. Women's bellies were cut open and babies butchered in the hands of their helpless mothers. Around 250 people were murdered in cold blood. Of these, 25 were pregnant women who were bayoneted in the abdomen while still alive. Fifty-two children were maimed in plain view of their mothers, before being slain and beheaded. Evidence suggests that the Jewish Agency and the commander of the British ground troops were aware that the massacre was taking place, but no one intervened.

News of the massacre was circulated far and wide, and events were exaggerated to spread fear amongst the Palestinian population. The Zionist ploy worked and thousands of Palestinians began to flee for their lives, leaving their homes and belongings behind.

Menachem Begin, a member of Irgun and a wanted terrorist by the British government (who later became prime minister of Israel), wrote:

"

Without what was done at Deir Yassin there would not have
been a State of Israel. (He added further): while the Haganah was
carrying out successful attacks on the other fronts…The Arabs
began fleeing in panic, shouting 'Deir Yassin'.

(Begin, *The Revolt*, p. 165)

"

The fate of Deir Yassin

Ironically, Deir Yassin can be seen from the Yad Vashem, the Holocaust
Memorial Museum. Deir Yassin is now called Givat Shaul Bet, a suburb
of the newly-created Greater Jerusalem. The streets in Givat Shaul Bet
are named after the murderous units in Irgun. The Palestinian cemetery
and mosques were all bulldozed to allow for roads and settlements for
exclusively Jewish use.

Towards creating Israel

13 December 1947: Zionists dressed in British army uniforms drove in front of a café in the Palestinian village of Yehiday. They stepped out of their vehicle armed with machine guns and randomly fired into the people gathered inside the coffee house. Some placed bombs next to Palestinian homes while others threw grenades at civilians. It seemed that a deadly massacre was about to take place, but a genuine British patrol arrived in time to cut short the well-organised killing spree. Without this intervention, the death toll of seven Palestinians would have been much higher.

Earlier the same day, six people were killed and 23 wounded when homemade bombs were thrown into a crowd of Palestinians standing near the Damascus Gate in Jerusalem. Another bomb in Jaffa killed six and injured 40.

18 December 1947: Two carloads of Haganah terrorists drove through the Palestinian village of Khisas, firing machine guns and throwing grenades. Ten people died in that attack.

19 December 1947: Five Palestinian children were murdered in the village of Qazaza when Zionist terrorists blew up the home of the village's leader.

1 January 1948: Approximately 200 Zionists armed with hand grenades and machine guns sneaked into the small village of al-Sheikh in the night. They attacked the houses on the edge of the village with hand grenades and then used machine guns. 40 people, mostly women and children, died.

13–14 April 1948: Zionists of the Lehi and Irgun paramilitary gangs entered the village of Naser al-Din during the night of 13 April dressed as Palestinian defenders. When local people went to greet them, the terrorists opened fire and killed all but 40 people. All houses in the village were razed to the ground.

21 May 1948: After several failed attempts to occupy the village of Beit Daras, Zionists mobilised a large contingent of fighters to surround the village. Villagers decided that the women and children should leave the village, but they were massacred as they attempted to flee.

11 July 1948: After the Israeli 89th Commando Battalion led by Moshe Dayan occupied Lydda, the Israelis instructed the Palestinians to proceed to the Dahmash Mosque where they would be safe. In retaliation for a hand grenade attack that killed several Israeli soldiers after the surrender, 80–100 Palestinians were massacred in the mosque; their bodies lay decomposing for 10 days in the mid-summer heat.

News of the massacre spread fear and panic among the Palestinian population of Lydda and Ramle, who were ordered to leave after Zionist soldiers had confiscated their personal belongings. Yitzhak Rabin, the Brigade Commander in charge, later said:

66

There was no way of avoiding the use of force and
making the inhabitants march 10–15 miles to the point where
they met up with [Jordan's Arab] legion.
(Kidron, Truth Whereby Nations Live, p. 92)

99

Most of the 60,000 inhabitants of Lydda and Ramle evacuated to refugee camps near Ramallah; there were approximately 350 deaths caused by dehydration and sunstroke en route.

29 October 1948: The testimony of a Zionist soldier who participated in massacres in the village of Dawayma states: '…[They] killed between 80 to 100 Arabs, women and children. To kill the children they fractured their heads with sticks. There was not one home left without corpses … One commander ordered a soldier to bring two women into a house he was about to blow up … Another soldier prided himself on having raped an Arab woman before shooting her to death'. (Quoted in Rokach, Israel's Sacred Terrorism, p. 18)

IRGUN ZWAÏ LĚUMI BE-EREZ JISRAËL
ORGANISATION MILITAIRE NATIONALE JUIVE D'EREZ JISRAËL
JEWISH NATIONAL MILITARY ORGANISATION OF EREZ JISRAËL

An Irgun poster for distribution in Central Europe.

18.3 Zionist Poster appealing for Jewish support

The above are a few examples from a long list of atrocities: Acre, Beisan, Beersheba, Haifa, Jaffa and Jenin saw extreme violence. There was no action or censure from the international community in response to the atrocities. Key individuals from amongst the terrorists became leaders of the Zionist state; they were described as 'statesmen' and 'men of peace'. Conversely, Palestinians who resisted, and continue to resist, the occupation are labelled as 'terrorists'.

The birth of a nation

On 14 May 1948, a group of Zionist terrorists wanted by Britain gathered in Tel Aviv and, led by David Ben-Gurion, declared the birth of Israel.

> **Who Created Israel?**
> It is wrong to claim that the UN created Israel. It was created by the violence and terrorist acts of the Zionist occupation.

Ben-Gurion wrote in *Rebirth and Destiny of Israel*:

66

Until the British left, no Jewish settlement, however remote was entered or seized by the Arabs, while the Haganah captured many Arab positions and liberated Tiberias, Haifa, Jaffa and Safad.

99

The Palestinians objected to the usurpation of their land. Not surprisingly, in response to the Zionist aggression Palestinians organised themselves to reclaim their territory and rights.

On 20 May 1948, the UN appointed Count Folke Bernadotte, the Swedish diplomat as a mediator between the Palestinians and Israelis.

The Israelis were delighted at Bernadotte's appointment; he had previously shown extreme compassion when he helped save over 20,000 Jews from Hitler's concentration camps. After careful observation, Bernadotte reported back to the UN on 16 September 1948:

> **"**
>
> It would be an offence against the principle of elementary justice
> if these innocent [Palestinian] victims of the conflict were denied
> the right to return to their homes while Jewish immigrants flow
> into Palestine, and indeed at least offer the threat of permanent
> replacement of the Arab refugees who have been rooted
> in the land for centuries.
>
> (*Progress Report of the United Nations Mediator on Palestine*)
>
> **"**

Bernadotte's Plan

1. Palestinians must be allowed to return to their homes in Palestine at any time.
2. If they choose not to return, they must be compensated in full by Israel for the losses they incurred.

The Zionists were furious at his suggestions, and Lehi (the Stern Gang) depicted Bernadotte as:

> **"**
>
> a Nazi agent and…concluded the task of the moment is to oust
> Bernadotte and his observers. Blessed be the hand that does it.
>
> (Stanger, 'A Haunting Legacy', p. 265)
>
> **"**

On 17 September 1948 Bernadotte and his French assistant, Colonel Serot, were assassinated. It is suspected that members of the Stern Gang carried out the assassination.

The Israelis were ruthless and eliminated anyone who obstructed the Zionist enterprise. Israel's apologists often depict the creation of Israel as a 'war of independence', wherein Israel is illustrated as 'David' pitched against the Goliath-like Arab forces of Egypt, Jordan, Syria and Iraq.

18.4 IDF forces in Beersheba, 1948

Myth

Israelis claim that in 1948 the Palestinians left their homes of their own accord and that the Arab leaders promoted this via radio broadcasts.

Reality

An Irish journalist found not a single appeal or order to leave from Arab leaders broadcast on radio. There was, however, evidence that Zionist stations broadcast in Arabic urging Palestinians to leave their homes.

(Childers, *The Spectator*, 12 May 1961)

In response to the intimidation and atrocities perpetrated by the Zionists against Palestinians, and the subsequent declaration of independence by Israel in May 1948; a combined military force from Egypt, Jordan and Syria marched into Palestine to protect the Palestinians and defeat Zionist aggression. In Righteous Victims, the Zionist historian Benny Morris records that at the beginning of this war Palestinians numbered around 28,000 troops, against 65,000 Israeli soldiers. However, by spring 1949, the Israelis had a massive force of 150,000 compared to 40,000 Palestinian troops. The Israelis were better trained (many by the British army during the Second World War), with superior military hardware and greater manpower. The result was a crushing defeat for the Palestinians and their allies; the Palestinians were humiliated by Israeli brutality and remained dispersed after defeat.

By the time a ceasefire was implemented some 10 months later, the Israelis occupied 78 per cent of historical Palestine, almost twice as much land as they had been allocated by the UN partition plan. More crucial in the long-term was the creation of the on-going Palestinian refugee crisis. The Israelis pushed the Palestinians out of their homes as they advanced into Palestinian land, and over 700,000 Palestinians became refugees. Palestinians call this 'al-Nakba' (the Catastrophe).

In December 1948, the UN passed Resolution 194 to establish a UN Conciliation Commission to broker peace between Israel and the Arab states. Israel objected to many of the Resolution's articles, and has failed to abide by them until the present time. After the UN asked Israel to allow Palestinian refugees to return to their homes and farms, Israel passed an 'absentee law', which allowed immigrant Jews to occupy the homes of Palestinians who had fled or were driven out during the war. The law placed the onus on the Palestinians,

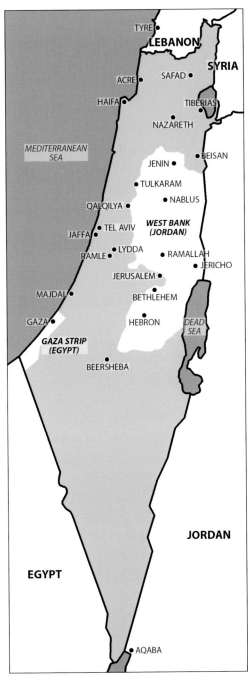

The Israeli occupied area, 1947–1948

the victims of the war, to prove that they were not absent. As many Palestinians could not meet this unduly heavy burden of proof the inevitable result, and design, of the **absentee law** was that immigrant Jews occupied all Palestinian homes, farms and businesses.

> **UN Resolution 194**
> Resolves that the refugees wishing to return to their homes and live in peace with their neighbours should be permitted to do so at the earliest practicable date, and that compensation should be paid for the property of those choosing not to return and for loss of or damage to property which, under principles of international law or in equity, should be made good …

Israel also implemented its apartheid **Law of Return of 1950**. This law provides an automatic right of Israeli citizenship to all Jews from anywhere in the world; whilst Palestinians, who are the legitimate owners of the land and property, continue to live as refugees since 1948 and are unable to return to their home.

Confessions of Ethnic Cleansing

"

'Jewish villages were built in the place of Arab villages. You do not even know the names of these Arab villages, and I do not blame you, because these geography books no longer exist; not only do the books not exist, the Arab villages are not there either. Nahalal arose in the place of Mahalul; Gevat in the place of Jibta; Sarid in the place of Huneifs; and Kefar Yehoshua in the place of Tal Shaman. There is not one place built in this country that did not have a former Arab population'.
(Moshe Dayan, *Ha'aretz*, 4 April 1969, quoted in Said, *The Question of Palestine*, p. 14)

"

CHAPTER 19

More Israeli Massacres
1949-1953

The Qibya massacre

On 14 October 1953, Ariel Sharon's Commando Unit 101 entered the village of Qibya by night and slaughtered the inhabitants. Up to 700 Israeli troops participated in the massacre; the killing extended to livestock.

Forty-two houses, the village mosque and school were dynamited. By morning, Israelis had killed all of the villagers; Sharon, a man whom in 2002 US President George W. Bush hailed as a 'man of peace' had murdered 75 innocent men, women and children.

The attack was bloody and one of the most brutal in this conflict. In *Righteous Victims*, Israeli historian Benny Morris writes that Sharon's unit received instructions to carry out 'destruction and maximum killing' in retaliation for a Palestinian 'terrorist' attack that originated elsewhere. According to Slater: 'the villagers were herded into their homes, which were then blown up'.

19.1 The ruins of Qibya

19.2 Palestinian victims of Israeli terror

Acting Prime Minister and Foreign Minister Moshe Sharrett wrote in his diary:

> 66
>
> I told Lavon that this [attack] will be a grave error, and recalled,
> citing various precedents, that it was never proved that reprisal actions
> serve their declared purpose. Lavon smiled…and kept to his own
> idea…Ben Gurion, he said, didn't share my view.
> (14 October 1953, quoted in Rokach, *Israel's Sacred Terrorism*, p. 23)
>
> 99

Two days later Sharrett wrote in his diary:

> 66
>
> I must underline that when I opposed the action I didn't even
> remotely suspect such a bloodbath. I thought I was opening one
> of those actions which have become a routine in the past. Had I even
> remotely suspected that such a massacre was to be held, I
> would have raised real hell.
> (16 October 1953, quoted in Rokach, *Israel's Sacred Terrorism*, p. 24)
>
> 99

Sharrett in the Cabinet

'[In the Cabinet meeting] I condemned the [Qibya] affair that exposed us in front of the whole world as a gang of blood-suckers, capable of mass massacres regardless, it seems, on whether their actions may lead to war. I warned that this stain will stick to us and will not be washed away for many years to come'.

(18 October 1953, quoted in Rokach, *Israel's Sacred Terrorism*, p. 24)

The Sharafat massacre

On 7 February 1951, Israeli soldiers crossed the armistice line and entered the village of Sharafat, 5 km from Jerusalem. The Israeli forces blew up the homes of the village leader and his neighbours. Ten Palestinians were murdered (including two elderly men, three women and five children) and eight were wounded.

The Kafr Qasem massacre

19.3 Victims of the Kafr Qasem massacre

At 4:00 pm on 29 October 1956, Israeli frontier guards started what they called a tour of the Triangle Villages. The Israelis reached Kafr Qasem at around 4:45 pm and informed the villagers the curfew was to start from 5:00 pm instead of 6:00 pm, as originally announced. The Palestinians protested that about 400 villagers were still working outside the village and that there was not enough time to inform them of the new timing. An officer assured him that they would be taken care of, and went to wait at the entrance to the village.

That evening, forty-three Kafr Qasem villagers were murdered in cold blood as they returned from work. Those killed included women and children.

The al-Sammou massacre

On 13 November 1966, Israeli forces raided the village of al-Sammou and destroyed 125 houses. The village clinic, school and 15 houses in a neighbouring village were also destroyed. Eighteen people were murdered and 54 were severely wounded.

Other Israeli massacres

o **Al-Tira (Haifa) massacre:** On 12 December 1947, 55 Palestinians were killed.

o **Yaheda massacre:** On 13 December 1947, 19 Palestinians were murdered and 73 wounded.

o **The Jaffa (ruins) massacre:** On 4 January 1948, 26 Palestinians were killed and dozens wounded.

o **The Semiramis Hotel massacre:** On 5 January 1948, 43 Palestinians were murdered by a bomb explosion in the hotel basement.

o **Jaffa Gate massacre:** On 7 January 1948, 25 Palestinian civilians were killed and dozens wounded.

o **Tantura massacre:** On 15 May 1948, more than 200 Palestinians were killed and 53 escaped.

o **Beit Daras massacre:** On 21 May 1948, a large number of women and children left the village. They were later surrounded by Israeli troops and murdered.

o **Safsaf massacre:** On 29 October 1948, 50 civilians were killed and the whole village was cleared of Palestinians.

o **Hula massacre:** On 31 October 1948, 85 civilians were murdered.

o **Al-Arqoub massacre:** In December 1948, 14 Palestinians were killed.

o **Gaza City massacre:** On 5 April 1956, 56 Palestinians were murdered and 103 injured.

o **At Khan Yunis Village and the adjacent refugee camp:** On 3 November 1956, more than 275 innocent people were killed.

CHAPTER 20

The Lavon Affair
1954

20.1 The Suez Canal

Gamal Abdul Nasser became Egypt's leader in 1952, while Ben-Gurion retired to allow Moshe Sharrett, a dove by Zionist standards, to become Prime Minister. Sharrett served as Prime Minister for only two years, from January 1954 to November 1955, when he resigned as a result of the 'Lavon Affair'. He was replaced by Ben-Gurion for a second term.

The Israelis became concerned when the British agreed with Nasser to stop patrolling the Suez Canal. Israel's view was that the absence of the British army in the Canal Zone would give the Egyptians an incentive to advance across the Sinai.

In 1954, Israeli military intelligence put into place 'Operation Susannah'. This was an offensive against Egypt whereby Egyptian Zionist Jews were recruited to plant bombs and carry out terrorist activities at the American and British embassies in Egypt, along with other buildings frequented by Westerners. The attacks were designed to appear to be perpetrated by 'Islamic fundamentalists', at this time the *Ikhwan al-Muslimin* (the Muslim Brotherhood). The orchestrated attacks were to 'prove' to the West that Nasser was harbouring terrorists and thus unable to protect Western interests. The aim of Operation Susannah was to force Britain to keep its troops in Egypt.

The conspirators were fortunately caught and brought to trial, but the impact of the failed operation in Israel was immense. In meetings with Prime Minister Sharett, Israeli Defence Minister Pinhas Lavon denied any knowledge of the plan but was forced to resign and the plot became known as the 'Lavon Affair'. The Israeli government tried to deflect blame by framing the entire episode as proof of Nasser's hatred for the Zionists; it was not until 1960 that Israel admitted its role in this 'false-flag' operation.

Fact

All historians agree that Nasser wanted peace with Israel and that he was forced to change his mind by continuous Israeli aggression. In January 1955 he wrote, 'Israel's policy is aggressive and expansionist… However, we do not want to start any conflict. War has no place in the constructive policy which we have designed to improve the lot of our people. We have much to do in Egypt…A war would cause us to lose… much of what we seek to achieve'.

(Morris, *Righteous Victims*, p. 267)

Having failed to mobilise world hatred for the Egyptians and Palestinians, the Israelis continued their campaign of systematically slaughtering Palestinians and expropriating land. On 28 February 1955, Israel executed 'Operation Black Arrow' in Gaza, in which they destroyed the railway station and killed 40 Egyptians and 30 Palestinians.

There is an excerpt from Israeli Prime Minister Moshe Sharrett's personal diaries, in May 1955 he explains Moshe Dayan's strategy:

> **"**
>
> [Israel] must see the sword as the main, if not the only, instrument with which to keep its moral high ground and to retain its moral tension. Towards this end it may, no—it must—invent dangers, and to do this it must adopt the method of provocation-and-revenge … And above all—let us hope for a new war with Arab countries, so that we may finally get rid of our troubles and acquire our space.
>
> (Rokach, *Israel's Sacred Terrorism*, p. 47)
>
> **"**

CHAPTER 21

The Occupation of the Sinai
The Suez Crisis 1956

Between 14 and 22 October 1956, at a secret location outside Paris, David Ben-Gurion, French Premier Guy Mollet, and British Minister of State for Foreign Affairs Selwyn Lloyd met. This was in response to Nasser's nationalisation of the Suez Canal, a vital link between the Mediterranean and the Red Sea. The three men agreed to attack Egypt and take over the Suez Canal and the Sinai Desert.

> ### Suez Canal
> Nasser nationalised the Suez Canal on 26 July 1956.

Britain and France were to play the role of international 'police' when Israel initiated the attack. According to the plan, Israel was to attack and advance into Egypt, at which point Britain and France would offer the international community the 'service' of separating the two warring factions and safeguarding the Suez Canal. For further reading, see Benny Morris' *Righteous Victims* (pp 289–291).

> ### Death toll
> o   Over 2,000 Egyptians were killed.
> o   4,000 Egyptians were taken prisoner.
> o   Israel lost 190 soldiers.

As planned, Israel attacked Egypt on 29 October 1956 and rapidly advanced towards the Suez Canal. The Anglo-French 'police force' attacked Egypt on 5 November, a few days later than had originally been planned, to purportedly safeguard the Suez Canal. The Anglo-French forces headed for Port Said, but the US and the Soviet Union applied diplomatic pressure to end the advance. The UN called for a ceasefire on 7 November, when the Anglo-French forces were only 160 km away from the Canal. This ended direct Anglo-French involvement in the conflict.

CHAPTER 22

The Six-Day War
1967

> **Myth**
>
> As the Jews ploughed their fields and enjoyed the Mediterranean breeze, 200 million Arabs attacked Israel in order to drive its occupants into the sea.

Did the Egyptians actually start the 1967 War, as most of us are led to believe? Former Commander of the Israeli Air Force General Ezer Weizman, regarded as a 'hawk', stated:

> 66
>
> ...there was no threat of destruction against the existence of the State of Israel. This does not mean … that one [should refrain] from attacking the Egyptians, the Jordanians and the Syrians. Had we not done that, the State of Israel would have ceased to exist according to the scale, spirit, and quality she now embodies.
>
> (*Ma'ariv*, 19 April 1972, quoted in Chomsky, *Masters of Mankind*)
>
> 99

Menachem Begin, former Prime Minister of Israel, said:

> 66
>
> In June 1967, we again had a choice. The Egyptian army concentrations in the Sinai approaches do not prove that Nasser was really about to attack us. We must be honest with ourselves. We decided to attack him.
>
> (Chomsky, *The Fateful Triangle*, p. 100)
>
> 99

Moshe Dayan, Defence Minister in 1967, gave the order to conquer the Golan Heights. Many of the skirmishes with Syria were deliberately provoked by Israel and the kibbutz residents, who pressed the government to take the Golan Heights. Dayan stated:

> **66**
>
> We would send a tractor to plough some area where it wasn't possible to do anything, in the demilitarized area, and knew in advance that the Syrians would start to shoot. If they didn't shoot, we would tell the tractor to advance further, until in the end the Syrians would get annoyed and shoot. And then we would use artillery and later the air force also, and that's how it was ... The Syrians, on the fourth day of the war, were not a threat to us.
>
> (Schmemann, *The New York Times*, 11 May 1997)
>
> **99**

General Yitzhak Rabin (Israeli Chief of Staff, 1967):

> **66**
>
> I do not think Nasser wanted war. The two divisions which he sent to the Sinai, on May 14, would not have been sufficient to start an offensive against Israel. He knew it and we knew it.
>
> (Hammond, *Foreign Policy Journal*, 4 July 2010)
>
> **99**

> **66**
>
> The Israeli Defence Forces' (IDF) intelligence had concluded, only a few weeks before in its annual 'national strategic assessment', that war was highly unlikely in the near future.
>
> (Morris, *Righteous Victims*, p. 302)
>
> **99**

22.1 Destruction of the Egyptian air force on the ground

> **Death Toll**
> o   13,300 Arabs and 779 Israelis were killed.
> o   For every Israeli killed, 17 Arabs died.
> o   On the Egyptian front: 338 Israelis and 12,000 Egyptians were killed.
> o   On the Jordanian front: 300 Israelis and 800 Jordanians were killed.
> o   On the Syrian front: 141 Israelis and 500 Syrians were killed.
> o   Israel took over 6,000 prisoners.

Attack on the *USS Liberty*

On the fourth day of the 1967 Arab-Israeli war, the intelligence ship, *USS Liberty*, was sailing in international waters 24 km north of the Sinai Peninsula. At 8:00 am on 8 June 1967, eight Israeli jets flew over the *Liberty*, which was flying a large American flag.

At 2:00 pm, waves of low-flying Israeli fighter-bombers repeatedly attacked the American vessel with rockets. The *Liberty* was left ablaze, listing sharply. In the first strike, eight of her crew lay dead and 100 seriously wounded, including the captain, Commander William McGonagle.

At 2:24 pm, three Israeli torpedo boats attacked the burning *Liberty* killing 25 more Americans, and Israeli gunboats circled the wounded ship firing at crewmen trying to fight the fires.

At 3:15 pm, the crew was ordered to abandon ship. Israeli warships closed in and poured machine-gun fire into

22.2 *The* USS Liberty, *hit by an Israeli torpedo*

the crowded life rafts, sinking two. As American sailors were being massacred, a rescue mission by the US Sixth Fleet carrier aircraft, USS Saratoga, was aborted on orders from the White House. The Israeli attacks killed 34 US seamen and wounded 171 out of a crew of 297.

> **US Naval losses**
> This was the worst loss of life suffered by US naval personnel from hostile action since the Second World War.

Aside from customary naval investigations, there was never any official investigation into this attack, which Israel claimed was a case of 'mistaken identity'. Survivors of the attack have sought legal recourse, but they have been unsuccessful. There are unanswered questions regarding successive US governments' efforts to protect itself and Israel from condemnation regarding the events of that day.

In *Body of Secrets*, James Bamford suggests that the *Liberty* had chanced upon the Israelis slaughtering Egyptian prisoners in the town of El-Arish, in the shadow of a mosque whose minaret could be seen by the crew and was being used as a navigation aid. Bamford's assertion is that although Israeli naval headquarters had clearly identified the *Liberty* as a USA ship, the attack was launched to cover up Israeli atrocities in El-Arish.

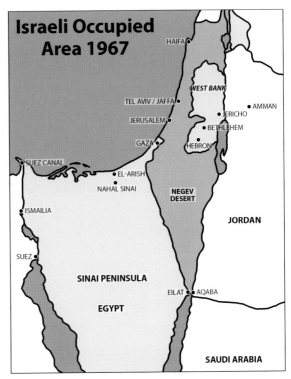

Israel committed many atrocities during the 1967 war, including the 'deliberate cold-blooded killing of unarmed UN soldiers' as well as the murder of Egyptian prisoners.

After the Six-Day War

In November 1967 the UN passed Resolution 242, instructing Israel to withdraw from the land it had occupied as a result of the 6 day war. Israel failed to comply.

From 25 to 27 June 1967, East Jerusalem and the West Bank were illegally annexed by the Israelis and declared to be part of Greater Jerusalem. The Israelis assumed control of the lives of over one million Palestinians, some of whom had escaped the clutches of the Zionists in 1948. Israel created a further 350,000 Palestinian refugees in the 1967 war.

22.3 Palestinians escaping across the River Jordan

Pushing the Palestinians out

Israel imposed military rule over the Palestinians; its policy was to employ oppressive tactics to force the Palestinians out of the newly occupied territories. Up to 350,000 Palestinians were expelled and forced into refugee camps in 1967. In September 1967, Joseph Weitz, architect of the transfer programme and deputy chairman of the JNF said:

> 66
>
> There is no other way but to transfer the Arabs from here to the neighbouring countries, transfer all of them, not one village or tribe should remain.
> (Karmi and Cotran, *The Palestinian Exodus*, p. 78)
>
> 99

Moshe Dayan said in November 1967:

> 66
>
> We want emigration…We want to encourage emigration according to a selective program.
> (Morris, *Righteous Victims*, p. 338)
>
> 99

Reality

'Israelis liked to believe…that they were running an "enlightened" or "benign" occupation… The truth was radically different…Israel's [occupation] was founded on brute force, repression and fear, collaboration and treachery, beatings and torture chambers, and daily intimidation, humiliation, and manipulation'.

(Morris, *Righteous Victims*, p. 341)

From 1967 to 1982, Israel's military government demolished 1,338 Palestinian homes on the West Bank. Over this period, more than 300,000 Palestinians were detained without trial for various periods by Israeli security forces.

In violation of international law, Israel confiscated over 52 per cent of the land of the West Bank and 30 per cent of the Gaza Strip for military use or for Jewish settlements only. Settlements are an Israeli symbol of authority and ownership over Palestinian land, what they still refer to as 'creating facts on the ground'.

1968

- o 21 March: The Israeli army attacks the village of al-Karameh in the Jordan Valley.
- o 26 December: Arabs shoot at one Israeli airliner in Athens.
- o 28 December: The Israelis blow up 13 Arab aircraft in Beirut.

1969

- o 11 March: Golda Meir, who infamously made the chilling statement 'there is no such thing as Palestinians', becomes Prime Minister of Israel.
- o 21 August: Al-Aqsa mosque is set on fire and the entire south wing was burnt down, including the precious *minbar* (pulpit) of Nur al-Din commissioned 700 years previously and installed by

22.4 The minbar of Salahuddin

Salahuddin al-Ayubi. The man found guilty sought refuge in a kibbutz and was set free after receiving psychiatric counselling.

1970

o 8 April: Israeli air strikes kill 30 schoolchildren in Bahr al-Bakr, Egypt.

o 6–12 June: Confrontation between the PLO and Jordanian forces begins, leading to 'Black September'.

1971

o The Palestine Liberation Organisation (PLO) are expelled from Jordan and move to Lebanon.

1980

o 30 July: Israel passes the *Basic Law: Jerusalem, Capital of Israel* that laid a claim to Jerusalem (East Jerusalem occupied in 1967 and West Jerusalem occupied in 1948) as being Israel's eternal and indivisible capital. This is rejected by the UN Security Council.

CHAPTER 23

The Yom Kippur War
1973

The Background

After Anwar Sadat was elected president of Egypt in October 1970, his first goal was to secure peace with Israel. In 1971, Sadat offered the famous peace treaty: to reopen the Suez Canal conditional upon a withdrawal of Israeli forces to pre-1967 boundaries. This was wholly rejected by Israel.

On 6 October 1973, which was the date of Yom Kippur (the holiest day in Judaism,) Egypt and Syria launched a surprise attack against the territory illegally occupied by Israel. For the first week Egyptian forces made successful advances and it appeared, for the first time, that Israel was not invincible.

The Egyptians managed to push the Israelis back from the Suez Canal, upon which Israel called on Ariel Sharon to take charge. From a military point of view, Sharon's ruthless nature paid dividends. In what was a brutal and savage advance, he pushed the Egyptian forces back and dispatched a Division to advance on Cairo.

The Americans became alarmed as Sharon got to within 100 km of the Egyptian capital. His advance brought the Americans, who were backing Israel, into confrontation with the Russians, who were supporting the Egyptians. In the climate of the Cold War, the threat of a nuclear conflict was a real possibility.

> **Myth**
> Israel claimed the Arabs tried to destroy Israel once and for all.
>
> **Reality**
> Arab armies only tried to regain the territory lost to Israel in the 6 day war and retained by it in breach of UN Resolution 242. They only attacked the Israeli army in the occupied territories.

As criticism of Israel's war conduct grew within the country, in April 1974 Golda Meir was forced to resign. The only Israeli hero was Sharon, who was carried shoulder high while the crowds chanted, 'Sharon, King of Israel'.

> **Sharon stated:**
> 'Israel is now a military superpower and nothing would happen if the Americans stopped sending Phantoms. All the forces of European countries are weaker than ours. Israel would conquer in one week the whole area from Khartoum to Baghdad and Algeria'.
>
> (Quoted in *The Times*, 23 October 1973)

> **Death toll**
> Over 2000 Israelis.
> Over 15,000 Arabs.

Sadat and peace

Feeling desperate, Sadat knew that only the US, the power behind Israel, could help to establish peace. In July 1972, to prove his worth to the new world superpower and with the aim of soliciting assistance from the US, Sadat expelled his Russian 'advisers'. The US government was not impressed and ignored his plea for help in establishing a peace treaty with the US's close ally, Israel.

Failing in his efforts at diplomacy, in 1973 Sadat started a war with Israel. On this occasion the US responded without delay. Within months the US

23.1 Anwar Sadat

had helped to end the aggression between Israel and Egypt; further, by 1975 the US had 'facilitated' a non-aggression treaty between the two countries. The negotiations were successful, in November 1977 Sadat was invited to give a speech in the Knesset, the Israeli Parliament.

President Sadat's speech to the Knesset

'I did not come to you to conclude a separate agreement between Egypt and Israel...I came here to you to build together a durable and just peace and to prevent any Arab or Israeli bloodshed...Israel has become an established fact recognised by the entire world [and] we welcome you to live among us in peace and security...[But Israel must] give up once and for all the dreams of conquest, and the belief that force is the best way to deal with the Arabs...Expansion will gain you nothing.

There are Arab territories which Israel occupied, and still occupies, by armed force. We insist on complete withdrawal from these territories, including Arab Jerusalem...Any talk about a just and lasting peace... while you occupy Arab land by armed force would be meaningless... peace cannot be achieved without the Palestinians...there is no use in refusing to recognize the Palestinian people and their right to establish a State and to return.'

('President Sadat's Speech to the Knesset',
20 November 1977, pp 172–178)

Finally, in September 1978, after years of effort by Sadat and with the direct assistance of the US, a peace agreement was signed at Camp David, brokered by President Jimmy Carter. But this was not peace with the Arabs, nor was there any relief for the Palestinians. The peace agreement was only between Egypt and Israel.

The price for this peace was high; Israel refused to recognise the Palestinians and Egypt was effectively prevented from helping the Palestinians. Peace with Israel meant that Egypt could not object to any future Israeli ambitions. Sadat was later assassinated by Egyptians who regarded him as a traitor.

23.2 The assassination of Anwar Sadat

CHAPTER 24

Israel Eyes Lebanon
1978-1982

> **The formation of the PLO**
>
> At its first summit meeting in 1964, the Arab League sponsored the formation of the Palestine Liberation Organisation (PLO) to represent the Palestinian people and achieve the 'liberation of Palestine' through armed struggle.

The Jewish state, as proposed by the Zionists in 1919 at the Versailles Conference, included what is now Southern Lebanon extending up to the Litani River.

> **Myth**
>
> Israel had to occupy Lebanon for security reasons due to PLO threats to attack the Galilee region.
>
> **Reality**
>
> Israel had planned the occupation of Lebanon before the PLO existed, and before any threat of occupation or conflict between Muslims and Christians in Lebanon. For Israel, the occupation of Lebanon was part of the Zionists' expansionist dream.

Ben-Gurion records in his diary entry for 21 May 1948:

> The Achilles heel of the Arab coalition is the Lebanon. Muslim supremacy in this country is artificial and can easily be overthrown. A Christian state ought to be set up there, with its southern frontier on the river Litani. We would sign a treaty of Alliance with this state. Then, when we have broken the strength of the Arab Legion and bombed Amman, we would wipe out Transjordan; after that, Syria would fall. And if Egypt still dared to make war on us, we would bomb Port Said, Alexandria and Cairo. We would thus end the war, and would have put paid to Egypt, Assyria and Chaldea on behalf of our ancestors.
>
> (Bar-Zohar, *Ben-Gurion: The Armed Prophet*, p. 133)

Ben Gurion's vision sets out clearly, especially in light of recent events, how the ambitions of Zionism can cost the blood and tears of thousands of innocent people.

Dayan's plan for Lebanon in 1954, as revealed by the diary of Moshe Sharrett, Israel's former prime minister, was clear:

> According to him [Dayan] the only thing that's necessary is to find an officer, even just a Major. We should either win his heart or buy him with money, to make him agree to declare himself the saviour of the Maronite population. Then the Israeli army will enter Lebanon, will occupy the necessary territory, and will create a Christian regime which will ally itself with Israel. The territory from the Litani southward will be totally annexed to Israel …
>
> The Chief of Staff supports a plan to hire a [Lebanese] officer who will agree to serve as a puppet so that the Israeli army may appear as responding to his appeal *'to liberate Lebanon from its Muslims oppressors'*.
>
> (Rokach, *Israel's Sacred Terrorism*, p. 34)

On 28 May 1954, Ben-Gurion stated:

> "
>
> Israel should provoke Lebanon's Muslims to attack Lebanon's
> Christians in the hope of igniting a Civil War in Lebanon.
>
> "

Beirut, the Paris of the East, becomes a shanty town

In April 1975, the Muslim majority in Beirut began to object to their government being controlled by the minority Maronite Christians. Muslims were gaining ground but the Israelis, determined not to miss a good opportunity, allied themselves with Saad Haddad. Haddad was the head of the Christian Phalange sect and a Major in the South Lebanese Army (SLA). The Israelis openly supplied arms, equipment and even manpower to the Phalange.

24.1 Beirut before the Israeli invasion

> **The Plan**
> Israel had set the stage for an occupation, and so they waited …

Haddad, with Israeli support, began to occupy Muslim villages to create a security belt along Israel's northern border. Haddad's expansion encroached upon Palestinian refugee camps and a direct conflict with the Palestinians ensued. On 11 March 1978, eight Palestinian commandos landed on an Israeli beach, hijacked a bus and headed for Tel Aviv. A gunfight resulted in the deaths of 34 Israelis and all eight Palestinians.

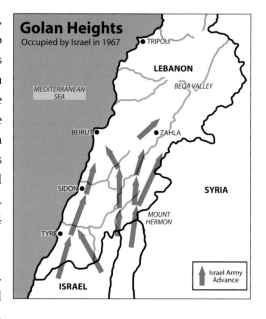

The Israeli army was ready to act. On 15 March 1978 Israel invaded Lebanon with over 20,000 troops, killing thousands of civilians and evacuating entire villages in the process. More than 100,000 Lebanese civilians were displaced.

In the face of international condemnation, Israel duly handed over the area they had occupied to the Phalange led by Major Haddad.

Over the next few years, Israel bombed PLO enclaves in Lebanon causing significant damage and loss of innocent lives. The PLO retaliated and in turn killed several Israeli civilians along the border. The US brokered a peace deal between Israel and the PLO, signed in July 1981.

Meanwhile, Ariel Sharon worked against peace. He continued to plan a means of occupying Lebanon, destroying the PLO and to gain more territory for Israel. Thus, in January 1982 Sharon secretly visited Lebanon to meet Bashir Gemayel, who was a candidate in the Lebanese presidential elections scheduled for August of that year. Sharon not only provided Gemayel with financial aid, but the two agreed upon a planned invasion of Lebanon to exterminate Muslims and the PLO.

The PLO resisted provocation and maintained its truce with the Israelis. Frustrated, Israel approached the US for permission to invade Lebanon in 1982, ostensibly in retaliation for a series of PLO attacks. The Americans could not be persuaded because all acts referred to were carried out in Lebanese territory, where Israeli soldiers had no legal right.

On 3 June 1982, the Palestinian faction led by Abu Nidal, which was by now aligned to Iraq, murdered the Israeli ambassador in London. It was obvious that neither the PLO nor the Lebanese had anything to do with the ambassador's death. This did not deter Israeli Premier Menachem Begin and Ariel Sharon, who began beating the drums of war. 'Invade Lebanon' was the mantra.

> ### The US gives the go-ahead
> In mid-May 1982, the USA gave the green light for Israel to invade Lebanon. In his memoirs, US General Haig emphasised that he told Sharon that if Israel acted without due provocation the effect on the US would be 'devastating'.
>
> (Morris, *Righteous Victims*, p. 513)

In plain English, General Haig was telling the Israeli generals to first provoke, then annihilate the PLO.

On 4 June, Israel mounted a massive airstrike across Lebanon, including a strike at the centre of Beirut. It was not until late afternoon on that day that the PLO began to fire across the border into Northern Israel.

The Israelis mounted a ground attack with 200,000 troops, slicing through Haddad's area of control and decimating everything in their way. By 10 June the Israeli forces were on the outskirts of Beirut. They had flattened the ancient city of Kasbah and committed atrocities in the Palestinian refugee camp of Ein al-Hilweh, outside Sidon.

> **Ein al-Hilweh**
> When the Israeli forces surrounded the refugee camp they promised
> the occupants that whoever did not bear arms would not be harmed.
> The Palestinians were now familiar with the Israeli forces' mode of
> operation. True to form, the Israelis took seven days to kill each and
> every individual in the camp; the last man was killed on 14 June 1982.

On 8 June, Begin told the Knesset:

"

We are not interested in a war with Syria.

"

On 11 June Israel signed a ceasefire with the Syrians. Four days later, Begin
ordered the Israeli army to attack the 85th Syrian Brigade.

On 13 June 1982, Begin publicly stated that Israel had no intention of invading
Beirut. Before he had returned to his seat, television pictures showed Israeli
tanks on the streets of Beirut.

> **Rabbis preach Holy War**
> We must not overlook the biblical sources which justify this war [the
> 1982 war in Lebanon] and our presence here. We are fulfilling our
> religious duty as Jews by being here. So it is written: the religious duty
> to conquer the Land from the enemy.
> (Wright, *Facts and Fables: The Arab-Israeli Conflict*)

On 2 July, Arafat informed President Shafiq of Lebanon of his intention to
evacuate, but this did not stop the Israelis from intensifying their attacks on
Beirut:

o   9 August: Israel bombarded Beirut with 36 bombing missions.
o   10 August: Israel hit Beirut with 16 missions.
o   18 August: Beirut was bombarded with 72 missions.

24.2 Beirut after the Israeli invasion

The relentless Israeli attacks were objectionable to US President Ronald Reagan, who:

> 66
>
> … called Begin twice on August 12, protesting that the air raids were 'unfathomable and senseless', [and] demanding an immediate IDF cessation of fire …
>
> (Morris, *Righteous Victims*, p. 537)
>
> 99

Death Toll

o Between 30,000 and 50,000 Lebanese and Palestinians were killed in Israel's onslaught on Lebanon.

o Around 500 Israelis were killed.

CHAPTER 25

The PLO Evacuate Beirut
1982

Sharon's brutal and merciless campaign was successful. On 21 August 1982 nearly 15,000 PLO fighters began to depart from Beirut by sea, leaving their women and children behind.

25.1 PLO members leave Beirut

On 23 August, under Israeli influence, the Lebanese parliament duly elected Bashir Gemayel, Sharon's ally, as president. Gemayel's public claim was to unite Lebanon, and to achieve peaceful coexistence between the country's different religious groups. He told the Israelis:

> **"**
>
> Personally I shall always be with you. Politically, however,
> I shall opt for my father's neutral line.
>
> **"**

The Israelis were furious and summoned Gemayel to Israel. On 1 September 1982, an Israeli army helicopter flew him secretly to Israel to receive a stern warning from Begin. Begin ordered Gemayel to make the dreaded Major Haddad a minister. Gemayel refused, which proved to be a fatal mistake. On the fourteenth day of the same month, Gemayel was assassinated. Habib Shartouni, a member of the Syrian Social Nationalist Party and also a Maronite Christian, was arrested for the assassination and imprisoned.

One of Begin's ministers at the time, Professor Yuval Ne'eman, said:

> Thus Israel now has an excellent opportunity to establish a
> new order in Lebanon…The Israeli Defence Force must be prepared
> for a long stay in Lebanon…It is perhaps also possible to
> integrate the strip south of the Litani.
> (Nakhleh, *Encyclopaedia of the Palestine Problem*, p. 153)

The Sabra and Shatila massacres

25.2 The Sabra and Shatila massacre

Between 15 and 18 September 1982, Israel's Minister of Defence, Ariel Sharon, and one of his generals, Rafael Eitan, dispatched the Lebanese Christian Phalange militia into the two Palestinian refugee camps of Sabra and Shatila, with orders to eradicate all Palestinian refugees. While the Phalangists were committing gross atrocities and massacres, Israeli forces sealed off the camps to stop those inside from escaping and those outside from offering assistance.

The International Committee of the Red Cross stated that 2,750 people were killed in Sabra and Shatila. The real number is thought to be much higher and may never be known.

25.3 Palestinian victims, Sabra and Shatila

Genocide (UN resolution 521)

On 19 September 1982, the UN passed Resolution 521 stating it was 'Appalled at the massacres of Palestinian civilians in Beirut' and 'Condemns the criminal massacre of Palestinian civilians'. Later, on 16 December, the UN qualified the Sabra and Shatila massacres as 'an act of genocide', recalling that 'genocide is a crime under international law which the civilized world condemns, and for the commission of which principals and accomplices—whether private individuals, public officials or statesmen, and whether the crime is committed on religious, racial, political or any other grounds—are punishable'.

While innocent Palestinian women, children and old men were being murdered, the Israeli Knesset assumed ignorance. The war criminal bearing most responsibility for the massacres that took place at Sabra and Shatila refugee camps is Ariel Sharon. Israel's own investigative body, the Kahan Commission, found Sharon responsible for the massacres and further recommended that Sharon be removed from public office.

Israelis in their tens of thousands took to the streets in 1982 in protest at Sharon's actions, only to elect him by tens of thousands of votes as their Prime Minister in 2001.

CHAPTER 26

The First Intifada
1987-1991

> **Intifada**
> Means 'an uprising or shaking off' in this case,
> shaking off Israeli occupation.

Causes

Since the Israeli occupation of Palestine first began, the Palestinians had considered a number of options to restore the freedom they once had. First, they turned to their neighbouring Arabs for assistance, and then to Yasser Arafat after 1967. The Palestinians then turned to the UN and the institutions created to uphold and enforce international law, and after that they turned to the diplomatic influence of the US. Nothing seemed to work.

26.1 Palestinian youth arrested by Israeli police

o   The Palestinians living in the territory occupied by Israel in 1967 became stateless and were treated brutally by the Israelis, suffering discrimination and inequality.
o   They earned half of what Israelis earned for a comparable job.
o   They had to pay a higher rate of tax.
o   Even after paying more in taxes, Palestinians did not benefit from the same level of medical or social services afforded to Israelis.
o   The Israelis illegally confiscated over 30 per cent of Palestinian arable land between 1967 and 1987.

- Palestinians suffered daily harassment and arrest, usually without cause.
- Beatings of Palestinians became routine.
- Palestinians were subject to daily document and body searches accompanied by verbal and physical abuse.
- Thousands of Palestinians were arrested and detained for weeks or months without trial. Between 1967 and 1987, 535,000 Palestinians were arrested by the Israelis.
- Most homes in refugee camps (where many Palestinians continue to live) had no running water and open sewers coursed through the streets.
- Palestinians required permits to travel, open businesses and construct houses, which Israel in most cases did not grant.
- Palestinian farmers were restricted from growing produce that would compete with Israeli farmers.
- Illegal Jewish settlers in the West Bank kept increasing: 35,000 in 1984, 64,000 in 1988, 130,000 in 1994 and over 200,000 in 2003.

26.2 An open sewer in a Palestinian refugee camp, southern Gaza

Myth

The world has often been told that the Arabs 'want to drive the Jews
into the sea', hence prompting the excuse of Israeli national security to
justify the country's illegal excesses.

Reality

o   October 1982: Cabinet Minister Mordechai Zippori proclaimed:
    'Don't worry about the demographic density of the Arabs. When
    I was born in Petah Tikva, we were entirely surrounded by Arab
    villages. They have all since disappeared'.

o   July 1987: Deputy Defence Minister Michael Dekel publicly called
    for the transfer of Palestinians to Jordan.

o   Minister Yosef Shapira proposed offering US $20,000 to
    Palestinians wishing to emigrate.

Jewish settlers moving into the
occupied territories continued to
increase. From 1967 to 1977, the
annual average was 770; between
1977 and 1987 this increased to 5,960
annually.

26.3 Israeli police brutality towards a Palestinian man

Currently over half of Palestinians are forced to live in sub-human conditions., which would not be considered fit for animals.

With Yasser Arafat and the PLO living in exile in Tunisia, the Palestinians were without leadership and vulnerable. A dynamic figure then emerged: Sheikh Ahmed Yassin mobilised the Palestinian community into action against the brutal and inhumane Israeli occupation.

The spark

26.4 An Israeli prison

On 8 December 1987, an Israeli Defence Force (IDF) truck crashed into a Palestinian car in Gaza, killing four civilians. The riots that broke out during the funerals were the catalyst for the first Intifada, a protest movement based on a combination of civil disobedience and active resistance. Palestinian protestors would boycott Israeli government institutions, refuse to work in

Israeli settlements, refuse to pay taxes, daub graffiti on Israeli buildings, set up barricades and throw stones at the IDF.

What did the Palestinians want?
First and foremost, Palestinians wanted to free themselves from the brutal Israeli occupation in accordance with the right of self-determination granted to them under international law. The Israelis rejected this as a ridiculous goal and clamped down even harder on the Palestinians. The Israelis deployed thousands of troops in Gaza and the West Bank, shooting and beating the Palestinian protestors indiscriminately.

> **Spiritual leader imprisoned**
> On 18 May 1989, the Israelis arrested Sheikh Ahmed Yassin, the spiritual leader of the Islamic resistance movement, Hamas, who was disabled from the neck down. Yassin was sentenced to life imprisonment (with his son to care for him), though he was released in 1997 in exchange for two Mossad agents.

The Intifada effectively lasted until October 1991, when the Madrid Peace Conference was convened. The Intifada was officially ended in September 1993, a period during which Israeli brutality was all too clear:

o   Over 50,000 Palestinians spent time in Israeli prisons, more than 20,000 of them without trial for periods of six months and more.
o   People caught throwing stones causing no injury were imprisoned for 3–6 months.
o   Those imprisoned included children as young as 12. Anyone under 12 was given a heavy fine, which had to be paid by parents.
o   The Israelis resorted to collective punishments, illegal under international law, and sealed off entire neighbourhoods, cutting off water and electricity supplies.
o   The houses of resistance fighters were demolished as a matter of routine.
o   66 Palestinians were deported from their own country.

Two examples of 'justice', Israeli style

1. On 22 August 1988, four Israeli soldiers chased a suspected stone thrower into a house and proceeded to beat and arrest the owner, Hani al-Shami, before taking him to an IDF camp where other soldiers took turns to beat him. An Israeli doctor was called and, after an examination, pronounced al-Shami to be healthy and not in need of treatment. Hani al-Shami later died of his injuries. Nobody was ever charged for his death.

2. Colonel Ya'akov Sadeh, Israel's deputy commander in the Gaza Strip Division, confessed to shooting a stone thrower in the neck, killing him instantly. Sadeh was found guilty in court, but was given only a six-month suspended prison sentence.

> **Israeli freedom of speech**
> Tel Aviv University invited two Arab lawyers from Gaza to give a lecture in the spring of 1988. During the presentation the Arab lawyers stated that peaceful coexistence can only be achieved by having two separate states; both lawyers were immediately arrested and sentenced to six months in prison.

Although the PLO had absolutely no involvement in the Intifada, the Israelis carried out unjustifiable acts of violence against PLO members outside Israel. Israeli agents murdered a PLO officer in Limassol, Cyprus, in a car bombing and assassinated Yasser Arafat's second in command, Khalil al-Wazir ('Abu Jihad') in Tunis in the presence of his wife and children.

> **Death toll during the first Intafada**
> *   Over 1,095 Palestinians killed.
> *   Over 15,000 Palestinians injured.
> *   Over 100 Israelis killed.
>
> (Figures from Israeli NGO - *B'tselem*)

CHAPTER 27

Towards the Peace Process
1991-1995

The Madrid Conference, October 1991

27.1 The Madrid Conference, 1991

When Saddam Hussein attacked Kuwait on 2 August 1990, the chairman of the PLO, Yasser Arafat, lent his support to the Iraqi leader. As a direct result, more than 300,000 Palestinians were expelled from Kuwait.

Further, since the beginning of the Intifada, an Islamic leadership had emerged within Palestine. The uprising began to be perceived by Israel as a Muslim-led struggle rather than a popular movement.

Faced with a strengthening grass roots resistance in Palestine, Israel blamed the Palestinian organisations Hamas and Islamic Jihad. In a move to check the growth of the Islamic resistance, Israel with the aid of America, sought to bring Yasser Arafat and the PLO in from the cold. For Arafat this was a lifeline to return to Palestine, and it was against this backdrop that the Madrid Conference was held.

Nothing tangible was achieved at Madrid, but it was the first time the two sides had formally come together to resolve the crisis. The only fruitful outcome was the decision to meet again.

In 1992, Yitzhak Shamir lost the Israeli election to ex-general Yitzhak Rabin. In the United States, Bill Clinton was elected president over George Bush (senior), and took office in January 1993.

Even after the Madrid conference, the Intifada raged on. Rabin believed that Islamism was on the ascendancy, and that the dominance of the US (now the only global superpower after the collapse of the Soviet Union) would not last forever. The possibility of Arab states obtaining nuclear weapons was growing. Rabin believed it was time to derive maximum benefit for Israel by negotiating directly with the PLO.

Towards Oslo

Two men were instrumental in bringing about the Oslo Peace Process, otherwise known as the Declaration of Principles (DOP). In December 1992 Yair Hirschfeld, a lecturer at Haifa University, and Abu Alaa (also known as Ahmed Qurei), head of the PLO's Economic Department, met secretly in London with the consent of both the PLO and the Israeli government.

The two men met a number of times, with the venue later switching to the Oslo home of Johan Jorgen Holst, Norway's Minister of Foreign Affairs in Oslo. The two men came up with a proposal that took everyone by surprise: the creation of a Palestinian interim self-government with responsibility for the administration of the territory under its control, and the withdrawal of the IDF from parts of the Gaza Strip and West Bank.

Whilst these discussions were taking place, the Palestinians were continuing to suffer as a result of the Intifada. In December 1992 eight Israeli soldiers were killed, which resulted in the arrest of approximately 1,600 Palestinians. Of these, 415 so-called 'Islamic fundamentalists' were expelled into the no man's land between Israel and Lebanon, where they languished in basic conditions for over a year.

> **Forced expulsion**
> Of the 415 so-called 'Islamic fundamentalists' expelled by Israel, 15 were Christians.

By January 1993, the Intifada was under the sole control of the Islamic groups, with members armed only with knives and stones against Israeli tanks and helicopter gunships. Rabin took draconian measures to end the Intifada and sealed off all access to, from and between the Palestinian territories.

In July 1993 Israel launched 'Operation Accountability' with heavy air and artillery bombardment of Southern Lebanon; the target was Hizbullah, the Shia militia. This resulted in over 300,000 villagers losing their homes. Hizbullah guerrillas retaliated. A truce was called on 31 July.

This was the background on the ground, when on 19 August 1993, Israeli Premier Shimon Peres went to Oslo to witness the Declaration of Principles (DOP). The DOP established a framework that would resolve the Israel–Palestinian conflict. Peres then flew to Washington and briefed President Clinton.

Before the participating parties could sign the DOP, they had to formally recognise each other's status:

> **Mutual recognition**
>
> Arafat stated: 'The PLO recognises the right of the state of Israel to exist in peace and security'.
>
> Rabin stated: 'The government of Israel has decided to recognise the PLO as the representative of the Palestinian people and to negotiate with it'.
>
> **Inequality**
>
> The recognition was, however, unfair because one party was a state, the other simply an organisation.

On 13 September 1993, under the watchful eye of President Clinton, Peres and Arafat signed the DOP on the White House lawn.

What is the Declaration of Principles?

The 'Declaration of Principles on Interim Self-Government Arrangements' was an attempt to set up a framework to resolve the continuing Israel–Palestine conflict. However, much of the text was open to unilateral interpretation by Israel. The thrust of the document was to provide:

o   The Palestinians with a 'self-governing' authority in parts of Gaza and Jericho (West Bank) for a period not exceeding five years. Full authority would be given thereafter.

o   Permanent settlement talks based on UN Resolutions 242 and 338.

o   So-called 'final status negotiations', which must start within three years (by December 1995) to include (amongst other points): the status of Jerusalem, the right of return of Palestinian refugees, Israeli settlements and security and borders.

o Gradual transfer of 'authority' over education, health, social services, direct taxation and tourism.

o The newly-formed Palestinian Authority (PA) would be allowed a police force whose main duty would be to prevent terrorism against Israelis from within PA areas; Israel would take care of all other external security matters.

o Israeli withdrawal from Gaza and Jericho by 13 December 1993.

o Israel's guarantee of safe passage between the two PA-controlled areas.

o Israeli responsibility for roads and its own security.

o The sea off the coast of the Gaza Strip to remain under Israel's control.

o Israeli civilians and military to continue to 'freely' use the roads in Gaza and Jericho.

o Israel given the right to pursue Palestinians throughout Palestinian-controlled areas.

Israeli goodwill

As a goodwill gesture, the Palestinians were allowed eight coastal police boats as well as two helicopters and four fixed-wing transport aircraft operating between Gaza and Jericho, all subject to Israeli air traffic control. Israel also agreed to release 5,000 Palestinians incarcerated in Israeli jails.

The agreement was flawed and unworkable. Israel took six months beyond the deadline of 13 December 1993, until 13 May 1995 in fact, to withdraw from the first two towns. Furthermore, Israel argued that it only had to hand over 15 square km of Jericho rather than the 150 square km the Palestinians had expected; eventually, the Palestinians were allowed 65 square km. Israel did not withdraw from Gaza until 18 to 19 May 1994.

> **The Masjid al-Khalil massacre**
>
> On 25 February 1994 (during Ramadan) Baruch Goldstein, a Jewish settler, entered the Ibrahimi Mosque during the Fajr (Dawn) prayers and began firing indiscriminately at Muslim worshippers with his Israeli army issued gun. Twenty-nine worshippers were killed in the attack and a further 125 wounded. The death toll eventually reached 69. The Israeli settlers' movement hailed Baruch Goldstein as a hero, and his grave is now a place of pilgrimage and annual 'celebration' for Jewish fundamentalist.

Yasser Arafat also faced a major problem as a result of the DOP. The Israelis wanted Arafat to arrest the leaders of the Islamic movement who were at the forefront of resisting the illegal Israeli occupation during the Intifada.

As attacks on their armed forces continued, the Israelis resorted to collective punishment by sealing off the occupied territories and preventing Palestinians from working in Israel. This resulted in more unrest in Gaza and Jericho as Palestinians began to view the DOP as an Israeli policy for containing Palestinian aspirations.

Oslo II was signed on 28 September 1995; it was an ambiguous agreement that superseded three earlier agreements signed after the DOP, which allowed for greater territory for Palestinians.

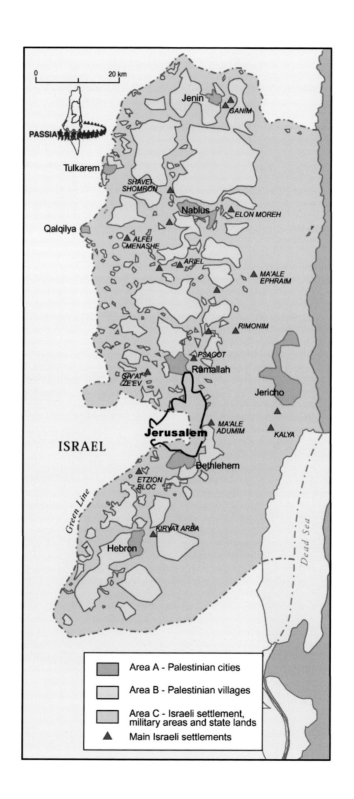

	Area A - Palestinian cities
	Area B - Palestinian villages
	Area C - Israeli settlement, military areas and state lands
▲	Main Israeli settlements

Zionist fundamentalists were unhappy with Rabin for recognising the Palestinians as a people and began to publicly compare him with the Nazis. Rabbis passed edicts of the death penalty to those 'who hand over' Jewish property or lives 'to the enemy'. Even Israeli politicians joined in the condemnation. Benjamin Netanyahu, a day before the Cairo Agreement was signed on 4 May 1994, said:

> In another hour Rabin will be able to announce that in
> Cairo he established the Palestinian terrorist state.
> (Morris, *Righteous Victims*, p. 635)

On 5 May, Zevulum Hammer of the NRP said:

> The terrorist organisations are being given a state on a silver platter.
> They are rejoicing over the blood of our sons and daughters.
> (Morris, *Righteous Victims*, p. 638)

Ariel Sharon directly linked Rabin's moves with the Nazis in order to appease his fundamentalist constituents:

> I never believed a day would come, when a Jewish government
> in Jerusalem would deal with selecting which Jews would be
> protected and which thrown to the dogs.
> (Morris, *Righteous Victims*, p. 635)

Thus Rabin's fate was sealed. On 4 November 1995, an extremist Jew assassinated the Israeli Prime Minister. The assassin later said that his intention was to put a stop to the peace process.

DOP: What do the experts say?

Yossi Beilin, an Israeli cabinet minister (1992–1996), initiated the 'secret channel' that led to the 1993 DOP and was a key negotiator:
'For Israel the main issue is security. This means that any future Palestinian state must be demilitarised…there will be no return to the 1967 borders…Palestinian refugees from 1948 will not be permitted into sovereign Israel…Jerusalem will not be divided…and Jewish settlements will not be uprooted'.

Hayder Abd al-Shafi, a Palestinian negotiator at the Madrid talks:
'Palestinians had made great sacrifices for a terribly flawed document that was phrased in generalities that read into it what was not there… Israel had no intention of ever allowing a Palestinian state…Given the terrible asymmetry in power between Israel and Palestinians the negotiators have been wrong'.

Nabil Shaath, the main Palestinian negotiator, admitted:
'Israel was not willing to commit in writing to any specific issue relating to settlements in the interim period'.

Ilan Pappé, an Israeli historian at Haifa University:
'The Oslo agreement is a wholly Israeli formula. There is nothing Palestinian in it…Through Oslo…Israel has succeeded in replacing one form of occupation with another'.

(Usher, *Dispatches from Palestine*)

CHAPTER 28

Leadership of Peace
1995-2000

After Rabin's assassination, Shimon Peres took over as Prime Minister for seven months until he lost to Benjamin Netanyahu in the election of May 1996. During Peres's premiership, Israel launched 'Operation Grapes of Wrath', a 16 day invasion of Lebanon between 11 and 27 April, in response to what Israel claimed, Hizbullah's Katyusha rocket attacks.

> **The Kfar Camp massacre**
>
> Over 400,000 Lebanese civilians fled from their homes within the first week of the launch of 'Operation Grapes of Wrath'. On 18 April Israel attacked a UN compound at Kfar Camp, near Qana in Southern Lebanon where many refugees had taken shelter, and killed 160 people.

The Netanyahu years, 1995–1999

When Benjamin Netanyahu came to power in the election of May 1996, the so-called peace process was placed on the back burner. From the outset, Netanyahu had made clear that he had no interest in pursuing the Oslo accord.

In what is considered a direct provocation of the Palestinians, on 24 September 1999 Netanyahu ordered the construction of a tunnel that would run along Al-Buraq Wall (the

28.1 A tunnel under the Old City, Jerusalem

'Western/Wailing Wall') of Al-Aqsa sanctuary. As expected, the Palestinians reacted against the physical desecration of their holy site and protested to protect the buildings within the main Al-Aqsa sanctuary. Over the next three months the Israelis killed 70 Palestinians and wounded hundreds more.

The Oslo Accords required Israel to withdraw from 50 per cent of the West Bank; Netanyahu offered only 13 per cent.

The Wye River Memorandum 15–23 October 1998

To bring Oslo to fruition, the Americans tried to bring the two sides together in October 1998.

> **Jonathan Pollard**
>
> Netanyahu told President Clinton that he would sign on the condition that the US released Jonathan Pollard, an Israeli convicted of spying against the Americans. Clinton dismissed this demand as ridiculous. Perhaps not; Pollard was almost pardoned on the last day of Clinton's presidency, his release was only prevented by the intervention of Clinton's security advisors.

In February 1999, Netanyahu refused to honour the agreement he had reached with the Palestinians. Some left-wing Knesset members threatened a vote of no confidence in their Prime Minister. Nervous, Netanyahu called for an election to take place 17 May 1999 rather than fulfil his promises to the Palestinians. He lost the election and was replaced by Ehud Barak.

Assaults on Occupied East Jerusalem under Netanyahu (1995-1999)

o   Construction work began at the Ras al-Amoud settlement to create 132 dwelling units on Palestinian land.

o   In Har Homa, 6,000 dwelling units were built to house 30,000 Jews.

o   Approval of the 'Master Plan' to link Ma'ale Adumim with Jerusalem, this included 20,000–30,000 inhabitants in an area of 60,000 dunums.

All of these actions were in contravention of UN resolution 242. They also breached the fourth Geneva Convention, which prohibits Israel, as an occupying power, from removing Palestinians from the occupied territories, or transferring Israeli citizens into the occupied territories.

28.2 The Palestinian mountain, Abu Ghnaim, 2 km from Bethlehem had over 60,000 pine trees and was host to several hundred species of wild animals and plants

28.3 Israel expropriated this mountain in 1991 and converted it into a Jewish-only settlement with the construction of 6,500 housing units, renaming it Har Homa

The Barak years, 1999–2001

Barak was hailed as the saviour of Oslo and a champion ready and able to deliver peace. In his inaugural speech, however, Barak struck a death blow to peace when he stated:

1. There would be no concessions on the West Bank; i.e. no return to the pre-1967 borders.
2. Jerusalem would remain as 'the undivided capital of Israel' under Israeli rule.
3. There would be no dismantling of Jewish settlements in Gaza and the West Bank, which would remain under Israeli rule.
4. Any Palestinian army would be severely restricted and no 'foreign armies' would be allowed west of the River Jordan.

> **Under 'generous' Barak**
> When Ehud Barak took office in July 1999, construction started on an estimated 1,924 new residential units in the Occupied Territories. In the first half of 2000 settlement construction grew by 96 per cent. Even more alarmingly, the Barak administration budgeted US $292 million for settlements in the year 2001.

28.4 Settlement construction

At the time of the signing of the Oslo Accords the illegal settler population, excluding those residing in East Jerusalem, numbered 110,000; in June 2000 it had reached 195,000. At the time of writing (2019) the illegal settler population in East Jerusalem is estimated to be over 215,000.

27.2 Bill Clinton, Ehud Barak and Yasser Arafat at Camp David

Barak's 'generous' offer at Camp David, July 2000

Although this was the first time that an Israeli government had been party to negotiations about the future of Jerusalem, a closer look at Barak's proposals illustrated the hollowness of the Israeli concessions:

[a] The West Bank and the Gaza Strip, captured by Israel in 1967. When the Palestinians signed the Oslo agreement in 1993 they agreed to recognise Israel as a state, accept a limited 22 per cent of historic Palestine and allow Israel to keep the remaining 78 per cent.

[b] 10 per cent of the West Bank is occupied by Israeli settlers, with nearly 70 illegal settlement sites. Palestinians are not allowed to pass through these settlements thereby creating Bantustans. Barak's offer did not include the dismantling of these illegal Israeli settlements. Barak further demanded the creation of areas of 'Temporary Israeli Control'.

[c] The 'Temporary Israel Control' concept means Palestinian land (marked in black) would remain under Israeli military control for an indefinite period.

[d] Barak's 'generous' offer: 80 per cent of the West Bank split by Israeli settlement blocks, bypass roads and roadblocks. Palestinians would neither have the right to control borders, nor move freely within this 'Palestine State'.

- In reality Barak only offered autonomy to Palestinians in East Jerusalem, where de facto autonomy already existed.
- Israel's best offer was 88 per cent of the West Bank, but 12 per cent of that (the Jordan Valley) would be leased back to Israel for 99 years. There were various formulae to resolve the land question, but it must be borne in mind that all percentages referred to West Bank territory outside what Israel regards as the Greater Jerusalem area.
- The Palestinians accepted a straight exchange of 3–4 per cent of land, with Israel keeping the large settlements of Ariel, Gush Etzion, Givat Zeev and Ma'ale Adumim plus the settlements inside East Jerusalem; Palestine also ceded sovereignty over the Wailing Wall and the Jewish Quarter of the Old City to Israel. In return, Palestine insisted that all other settlements should be abandoned and their residents return to Israel or to the agreed settlements.

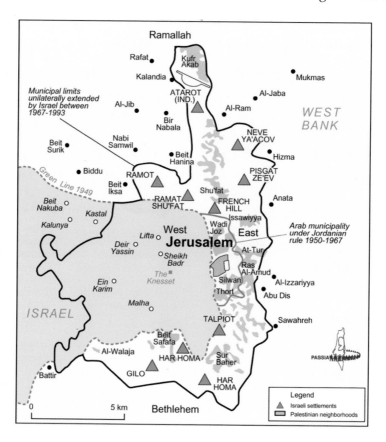

o   On Jerusalem, Israel offered a graded but 'constrained' sovereignty starting from the outside in. That is, Palestinians would have greater sovereignty over the outer suburbs like Beit Hanina and Beit Sahour, less so over areas like Sheikh Jarrah and Wadi al-Joz, and least over the Old City. In effect, there would be Israeli sovereignty over Jerusalem.

o   At first the Israelis resisted to negotiate about the holy places. However, under US pressure they proposed Israeli sovereignty over all holy places and Jewish rights of prayer at Al-Aqsa (with the warning that Israel reserved the right to build a synagogue at Al-Aqsa). The Americans compromised by suggesting Palestinian 'vertical sovereignty' over Al-Aqsa and Israeli control of what was underneath.

o   On security, Israel stipulated it must have the right to enter a future Palestinian state at any time it chose for security reasons. The Palestinians had already offered to consider the Jordan Valley a security zone for a period of six years; further, they had accepted demilitarisation and the presence of an international force and early warning stations on the West Bank. The Palestinians could not, however, accept unrestricted access into Palestine as a condition.

o   On refugees, Israel offered compensation but with no link to loss of property claims; there was no offer of restitution or admission of responsibility. A rumour circulated that Israel would accept the return of a token number of refugees to its pre-1967 territory, perhaps 100,000. Shlomo Ben Ami, Israel's Foreign Minister and chief negotiator at Camp David, said in an interview with the Israeli daily, Ma'ariv, on 6 April 2001 that these rumours were untrue: 'These reports were nothing but absolute lies. Never, not during any stage or under any circumstances did we agree to the return of refugees'.

In return for this package, Israel wanted Arafat to sign, in the name of the Palestinian people, an agreement that would mark the end of the conflict and to all outstanding Palestinian claims against Israel, including the much cherished right of return for refugees.

Israel was to keep strategic control over the West Bank and Gaza Strip including airspace, land borders, settlements and their transport routes to and from Israel. As an example, the settlement of Ma'ale Adumim, which is the largest in the West Bank and which Israel planned to annex as part of a final status agreement, would ensure that Israel controls all of traffic between the north and south of the West Bank. Under the proposed agreement, large Jewish settlement blocks in the Occupied Territories would be annexed into Israel. Moreover, Barak's supposed 'concessions' on Jerusalem would result in the expansion of Jerusalem's boundaries deep into Palestinian territory with the annexation of settlements like Givat Zeev to Jerusalem.

Evidently Barak, like his immediate Labour Party predecessors Yitzhak Rabin and Shimon Peres, used the Oslo process as a means to consolidate Israeli control over occupied Palestinian territories.

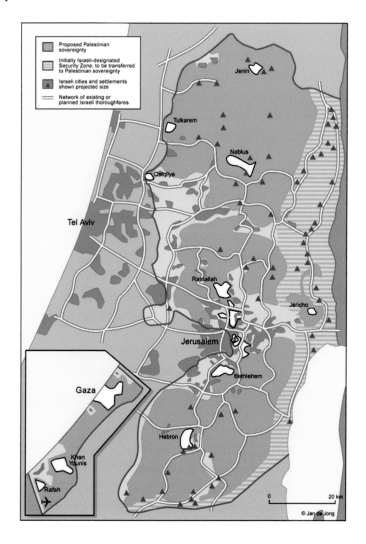

Myth

The signing of the Oslo Accords (the peace process) and a schedule for the resolution of final status issues would effectively end human rights abuses in the Occupied Territories and establish a Palestinian state.

Reality

5. The Oslo Accords did not end the Israeli occupation but, rather, enabled it to continue the occupation by other means. Oslo was a means by which Israel tried to replace the implementation and enforcement of the direct form of oppressive occupation with another, namely the Bantustan option. Oslo's leading principle, that of exchanging 'land for peace', did not amount to the end of the occupation. Israel still controls nearly every aspect of life in the West Bank and Gaza Strip through a strategic system of economic and geographic bottlenecks commonly termed 'checkpoints'.

6. The Oslo Accords effectively undermined the significance and applicability of international legal principles and key UN resolutions applying to the situation on the ground in the West Bank and Gaza Strip. It can be said that the Oslo Accords allowed the continuation of international law violations and human rights abuses against Palestinians.

CHAPTER 29

The Al-Aqsa Intifada
2000 -2004

29.1 Al-Aqsa Mosque

In September 1993 after the signing of the Oslo Accords, innocent Palestinians danced in the streets of Gaza, Ramallah and Jericho; and open-heartedly extended their hands for peace over the pain of the occupation.

Seven years later, the harsh reality of a flawed peace process came to fore. The result of the Palestinian awakening was the Al-Aqsa Intifada.

During the period between the signing of the Oslo Accords and the eruption of the Intifada, Israel violated every aspect of Palestinian life. Israeli abuses were the background to Sharon's provocative 'visit' to the Al-Aqsa mosque, the holiest Islamic shrine in Jerusalem, in September 2000 (accompanied by thousands of Israeli soldiers). In doing so, he deliberately lit the fuse of Palestinian frustration which led to the uprising.

Palestinian victims during Al-Aqsa Intifada
(29 September 2000–29 September 2004)

o   Killed: 3,334.
o   Injured: 52,000+.
o   Students injured: 4,090.
o   Schools shelled: 850.
o   Schools taken over as military bases: 8.
o   Schools taken over as detention centres: 25.
o   Deaths* at Israeli Checkpoints: 73.
o   Stillbirths* at Israeli Checkpoints: 9.
o   Births* at Israeli checkpoints: 43.
o   Journalists killed: 12.
o   Palestinian and foreign journalists injured: 470.
o   Foreign journalists killed: 2.
o   Attacks on ambulances: 409.
o   Arrests and detentions: 28,000.
o   Damage to residential buildings: 36,380.
o   Houses demolished: 12,099.
o   Living below poverty line – West Bank: 67 per cent.
o   Living below poverty line – Gaza Strip: 75 per cent.
o   Overall losses to Palestinian economy: US $10 billion.
o   Land destroyed: 6,500 hectares.

Sources: The Palestinian Red Crescent Society, the Ministry of Health, United Nations Children's Fund (UNICEF).

Statistics for two years.

Weapons used against Palestinians

1. Tear gas and stun grenades.
2. Rubber bullets.
3. Rubber-coated steel bullets.
4. Live bullets of various calibres.
5. Dumdum bullets.
6. M-16 and Galil rifles.
7. Heavy machine guns.
8. Nail bombs.
9. Artillery shells.
10. Armoured personnel carriers.
11. Tanks.
12. Surface-to surface missiles.
13. Air-to-surface missiles.
14. Apache and Cobra gunships.
15. F-16 and F-15 fighter jets.
16. Battleships.

CHAPTER 30

The Siege of Gaza
2004-2012

Israel leaves Gaza

The year 2004 was notable for a number of reasons: George W. Bush was re-elected as US President in November; and Palestinian leader Yasser Arafat died after a lengthy illness in the same month. Hamas's spiritual leader, Sheikh Ahmed Yassin, was assassinated by the Israelis earlier in the year. Palestine remained under attack from Israel throughout this period.

After Arafat's death, Mahmoud Abbas was elected Palestinian President. In an unexpected move Ariel Sharon, the Israeli Prime Minister, unilaterally decided to evacuate Jewish settlers

30.1 Mahmoud Abbas

from Gaza in late 2005 and destroy settlements. This was not the blessing for the people of Gaza it was made out to be; aerial attacks on Gaza by the Israeli Air Force increased and Israel imposed a blockade around the beleaguered Strip.

The democratic election of Hamas

In 2005, the US and European governments demanded that the Palestinians hold an election. The occupied territories went to the polls on 26 January 2006. To the surprise of pollsters in the West, Hamas won the election and schoolteacher Ismail Haniya became the Palestinian Prime Minister.

Independent international observers (including politicians from Europe and US) declared the election to be open and fair. Nevertheless, the Israeli and US government immediately announced that they would not deal with the democratically elected government of Palestine. The US, Europe and Israel imposed sanctions on Gaza (the stronghold of Hamas) and the Palestinian people for no other reason than that they had elected the 'wrong' government. The Israeli government withheld Palestinian tax revenue causing severe financial hardship to the Palestinian government, and intensified military attacks on Gaza. On 29 June 2006 Israel 'arrested' one-third of the Hamas-led Palestinian cabinet.

Israel's attack on Lebanon

In July 2006 Israel began an aerial bombardment of Lebanon after Hizbullah, one of Lebanon's political parties, captured two Israeli soldiers in a cross-border raid.

30.2 The Qana massacre, 2006

Following Hizbullah's raid and the abduction of the two IDF soldiers, Israel blamed the Lebanese government and launched an air and artillery bombardment, followed by a ground invasion. The West, led by the United States, did not immediately call for a ceasefire. The balance tipped after a horrific massacre at Qana in Southern Lebanon on 30 July 2006. The Israeli Air Force bombed a three-storey building killing 56 civilians, including 32 children; at which point the US secretary of State Condoleezza Rice belatedly called for a ceasefire. By then, however, over 1,000 innocent Lebanese civilians had been killed and over a million displaced.

In a repeat of previous responses, western governments were reluctant to place any blame on Israel, and attempted to incriminate Hizbullah. On this occasion, however, millions of people around the world recognised Israel's act of aggression. Professor John Mearsheimer, an acclaimed political scientist at the University of Chicago, commented that Israel had used the kidnapping of its soldiers as an excuse to attack Lebanon:

"

Israel had been planning to strike at Hezbollah for months ... Key Israelis had briefed the administration about their intentions.
(Milbank, *The Washington Post*, 29 August 2006)

"

The siege on Gaza intensifies

The attacks on Gaza continued and 18 Palestinian civilians were killed by Israel on 11 November 2006. The US vetoed a UN Security Council resolution condemning the attack and urging a swift withdrawal of Israeli forces from the area.

There were continuous Israeli attacks on Palestinians in both the Gaza Strip and the West Bank during 2007. The US began to fund and arm Abbas and his Fatah party, the main opposition political party to Hamas, hoping to create the conditions for a Palestinian civil war. In May 2007, just weeks after Hamas and Fatah agreed to run the National Unity Government, matters came to a head. A faction within Fatah, funded by Israel and the US, prepared to stage a military coup against the democratically elected Hamas government. Hamas struck pre-emptively and took full control over the Gaza Strip, ousting the militant Fatah activists. Although Hamas was successful in securing Gaza, this allowed Israel and its supporters to further tighten the blockade on the territory and bring its two million people close to starvation.

The situation worsened during 2008, when the Israelis imposed severe restrictions on the movement of people and goods at the Gaza border. Hundreds of students from Gaza were denied permission to leave to further their studies. Even acute patients were not allowed to go abroad for life-saving treatment.

'Operation Cast Lead' 2008

30.3 Israel's use of white phosphorous munitions in Gaza was internationally criticised

In late December 2008 Israel launched a bombing campaign against the Gaza Strip, followed by a full land invasion. After three weeks of bombing, more than 1,400 Palestinians had been killed. A further 40,000 people had been made homeless; and homes, schools, mosques and businesses had been destroyed. Munitions prohibited under international law (phosphorous bombs) were used against a civilian population. Phosphorous bombs were also used in an attack against a UN school in which Palestinians were taking shelter. Various human rights groups have produced detailed reports that denounce Israel for war crimes in Gaza.

This attack took place after 18 months of the blockade against the people of Gaza, imposed by Israel and followed by Western countries such as Britain and the US. By the end of December 2008, food and medicine stocks in Gaza were at an all-time low.

The blockade of Gaza has caused a humanitarian crisis, described by the Commissioner General of the UN Relief and Works Agency for Palestinians (UNRWA) as the worst she had ever seen. An international relief effort was launched which saw people from around the world working to ease the plight of the Palestinians. The BBC, succumbed to Israeli pressure when it reversed a decision to broadcast a televised charity appeal for Gaza. Claiming that to broadcast the Disasters Emergency Committee (DEC) appeal would breach the BBC's impartiality guidelines, or that there was 'concern about whether aid raised by the appeal could actually be delivered on the ground' (Thompson, 'BBC and the Gaza appeal').

Israel maintains its position that it had no option but to invade Gaza and destroy Hamas, because homemade rockets were being fired from Gaza into southern Israel. One town in particular, Sderot, became the focus of a media campaign to highlight these 'missile attacks'. Journalists were taken to see the effects on the town and population; yet, in a surprising disparity, the same journalists were forbidden by Israel from entering Gaza to report on Israeli attacks. Another omission was that Sderot itself was built on the ruins of a Palestinian town called Najd, whose population of more than 700 men, women and children were 'ethnically cleansed' by Jewish militias on 13 May 1948. Thus, the main cause of the ongoing conflict between Israelis and Palestinians, namely the ethnic cleansing of Palestine, was kept out of focus. The narrative remained that Israel was 'responding to Palestinian terrorism' and nobody dared to discuss the possibility that Palestinian resistance was to the illegal occupation of their land.

British political reaction to 'Operation Cast Lead'

Sir Gerald Kaufman (a Jewish British MP) said, 'Is it not an incontrovertible fact that Olmert, Livni and Barak are mass-murderers and war criminals … And they bring shame on the Jewish people whose star of David they use as a flag in Gaza'.

Peter Kilfoyle (former Labour Defence Minister) urged the government 'to ensure that no arms at all go to Israel at the moment, given that it is guilty in many people's eyes of state-sponsored terrorism with its activities in the Gaza strip'.

Sir Menzies Campbell (former Liberal Democrat leader) said, 'is not the blunt truth that … the Israeli Government persist in disproportionate military action … at a terrible cost to human life? If any other democratic state were behaving in that way, would we not by now be considering what other economic and diplomatic steps were available to us?'

Chris Mullin (former Foreign Office minister) said, "We should recognise … that these are war crimes that we are witnessing in Gaza, and start talking with our EU allies about organising sanctions and, at the very least, stop selling weapons to the Israelis, and perhaps talk about the withdrawal of our ambassador ".

('House of Commons Debate on Gaza', 12 January 2009)

The attack on the *MV Mavi Marmara*

Individuals and organisations around the world observed the crisis in Gaza with sadness and horror. In May 2010, an international flotilla of six ships set sail from Turkey, carrying desperately needed aid to Gaza. On 31 May Israel's navy boarded the MV Mavi Marmara and carried out a deadly raid which left nine Turkish nationals dead and several injured. Israel's actions were unprovoked, disproportional and, crucially, committed in international waters i.e. outside Israel's jurisdiction. Israel initially attempted to deny any wrongdoing. When its attempt was unsuccessful and pressure mounted, Israel in March 2013, apologised to Turkey and later provided compensation to the families of the killed peace activists.

30.4 The MV Mavi Marmara *comes under attack*

'Operation Pillar of Defense' 2012

30.5 A series of air strikes on Gaza

In November, Israel escalated its aggression by launching an assault on Gaza.

On 5 November, Israeli soldiers shot and killed an unarmed 20-year-old Palestinian man who approached a fence near Gaza's side of the border with Israel.

On 6 November, Israel struck targets in the Gaza Strip wounding five people, including four children. The Israeli strike damaged a mosque and a water tower.

On 10 November, the IDF shelled civilian targets in the Sa'ajiya area. Four teenagers aged 16 to 18 were also killed by an Israeli airstrike in a sports stadium while they were playing football.

Israel launched 'Operation Pillar of Defense' against the people of Gaza on 14 November, 2012. The offensive lasted for seven days before a ceasefire was negotiated on 21 November.

In the first strike of its brutal assault on Gaza, Israel assassinated senior Hamas leader Ahmed al-Jabari. He was killed despite being credited for maintaining peace between Hamas and Israel. Al-Jabari had, for example, been instrumental in securing the release of Gilad Shalit, the IDF soldier who was captured in 2006 and released five years later as part of a prisoner exchange deal.

The massacre of the al-Dalu family

30.6 Aftermath of the al-Dalu family bombing

On 18 November 2012, in the Nasser neighbourhood of Gaza, an IDF missile destroyed the al-Dalu's home. The attack killed 10 of Jamal Mahmoud's family members including five children and an elderly woman. Several nearby houses were also destroyed in the attack; resulting in the highest death toll of any single strike during the Operation. Jamal al-Dalu, the owner of the home attacked, was at the market at the time of the attack and survived.

Israeli authorities insisted that the target of the attack was Jamal's son, Mohammed, who was a member of al-Qassam (the armed wing of Hamas). Friends of the al-Dalu family and neighbours contradicted these allegations and maintain that Mohammed was a policeman working in the Hamas government. Israeli authorities also said that civilians had been warned to leave the area, but Jamal said that no warning had been given to allow his family to flee:

> **"**
>
> They didn't give us a warning. They just hit the house with the children in it. My daughters were in their youth. What did they do to them?
>
> (Rudorennov, *The New York Times*, 19 November 2012)
>
> **"**

The Palestinian Centre for Human Rights called the strike 'blatant targeting of civilians'. Human Rights Watch called the massacre a 'disproportionate' use of force and called for the perpetrators of the strike to be 'prosecuted for war crimes' and the surviving members of victims' families to be compensated.

The attack on the Shoruq media tower

Throughout the assault on Gaza, the Israeli Air Force continued to breach international law and human rights conventions in its targeted killing of civilians. The attacks extended to journalists and media offices including the Shoruq media tower. The tower housed journalists working for Palestinian and international media outlets. The strikes killed a two-year-old child and a Palestinian cameraman, as well as wounding 10 media workers.

30.7 The Shoruq media tower is attacked

The Israeli military's actions against civilians and journalists were condemned by international news organisations, including Reporters Without Borders (RWB). Christophe Deloire, Secretary-General of the organisation, said:

> 66
>
> … under humanitarian law, the news media enjoy the same protection
> as civilians and cannot be regarded as military targets … Attacks on
> civilian targets are war crimes and serious violations of the Geneva
> Conventions. Those responsible must be identified.
> (RWB, 18 November 2012)
>
> 99

Over the seven days of Operation Pillar of Defense, the IDF struck more than 1,500 sites in the Gaza Strip, most of which were civilian targets. The Palestinian Centre for Human Rights reported 102 civilians, 55 militants, one policeman, 30 children and 13 women were killed during the attack. Besides the killed, countless families had their homes destroyed and were left displaced.

The solidarity movement in the West Bank

While attacks were ongoing in Gaza, solidarity protests were being held across the West Bank; but such protests were brutally put down by the Israelis. On 18 November a 31-year-old Palestinian man, Rushdi al-Tamimi, was participating in a demonstration in Nabi Saleh and was killed by Israeli gunfire. Thousands attended his funeral and were fired upon by Israeli forces with rubber bullets and tear gas.

By 19 November, over 50 Palestinians were reported injured during solidarity protests held in East Jerusalem, Ramallah, Bethlehem, Beit Ummar and Qalandia. Further protests and clashes occurred throughout the West Bank between 21–22 November.

The IDF closed the entrance to Bani Naim after clashes between Israeli forces and the town's residents. Meanwhile, the northern West Bank village of al-Jalama was declared 'a closed military zone' after hundreds of Palestinian demonstrators protested at the village checkpoint. Five Palestinians were arrested in house raids by the Israeli military in Ya'bad and Tubas.

CHAPTER 31

One Step Forward, Two Steps Back
2013–2019

Peace talks again

On 29 July 2013, with the encouragement of US Secretary of State John Kerry, Palestinians and Israelis sat across the negotiating table in Washington DC for the first time since 2010.

From August to September 2013, the two sides attempted to come to an arrangement that would satisfy both the Palestinians and the Israelis; but by December 2013 little progress had been made. As a part of the peace talks, it was proposed that the Jordan Valley and border crossings into Jordan would be placed under Palestinian control, providing a Palestinian state with a border with Jordan. Elements in the Israeli government objected to this and put forward a bill to annex the Jordan valley, thus preventing Netanyahu from accepting this proposal. In January 2014 Israel approved plans for the construction of a further 1,400 Jewish settler homes in the West Bank and East Jerusalem (Lewis, *Reuters*, 10 January 2014). Disappointed, the chief Palestinian negotiator, Saeb Erekat, declared:

66

Israel is responsible for foiling the efforts of Kerry, [it] is a clear step toward apartheid … Israel wants to destroy the two-state solution through its daily practices.
(Abu Toameh, *The Jerusalem Post*, 30 December 2013)

The recent announcement shows Israel's clear commitment to the destruction of peace efforts and the imposition of an apartheid regime.
(Saeb Erekat, quoted in Lewis, 10 January 2014)

99

In March 2014, the release of 104 Palestinian prisoners, which was a precondition of the peace talks, was suspended by Israel after only 78 had been released. In the same month Netanyahu demanded Palestinian recognition of the Jewish State as a pre-condition of peace:

> "
>
> it's time the Palestinians stopped denying history…
> Just as Israel is prepared to recognize a Palestinian state, the
> Palestinians must be prepared to recognize a Jewish state. President
> Abbas, recognize the Jewish state, and in doing so, you would be
> telling your people, the Palestinians, that while we might have
> a territorial dispute, the right of the Jewish people to a state
> of their own is beyond dispute.
> (Netanyahu, *Haaretz*, 4 March 2014)
>
> "

Arafat and his Fatah organisation had already recognised Israel in the 1993 Oslo Accords. It was clear to the Palestinians that Israel's strategy was to demonstrate that it was interested in peace talks; whilst at the same time provoking the Palestinians and the Arab League to the point where withdrawal from negotiations was the only option. Commentators suggest that this is a reflection of Israel's broader aims in its relationship with the Palestinian territories:

> "
>
> Maintaining the status quo has not just been about restoring the
> military balance to the 'tolerable level of violence' but also about
> maintaining the broader status quo in the Israeli–Palestinian conflict…
> n which Israel maintained military superiority while the Palestinian
> body politic remained divided and stateless.
> (Schulze, *The Arab–Israeli Conflict*, p. 114)
>
> "

> **"**
>
> Recent Israeli strategy has been to postpone solution of the Palestinian
> issue and maintain the status quo, which has strengthened those
> who see this as an opportunity for one Jewish state between the
> Jordan River and the Mediterranean Sea. This makes it impossible for
> Israel to be both a Jewish and a democratic state, and
> makes continuing violence inevitable.
> (Carter, *USA Today*, 17 March 2016)
>
> **"**

On 23 April 2014 the rival Palestinian factions, Hamas and Fatah, signed an agreement to form a unity government within five weeks from that date and hold parliamentary elections by the end of the year. Israel suspended peace talks almost immediately, with Netanyahu blaming Abbas for the failure to achieve peace:

> **"**
>
> What has happened is a great reverse for peace, because we had hoped
> the Palestinian Authority [PA] president Abbas would embrace the
> Jewish state, the idea of two nation states, [a] Palestinian one and a
> Jewish one … But instead, he took a giant leap backward.
> (Black, Beaumont and Roberts, *The Guardian*, 24 April 2014)
>
> **"**

> **"**
>
> Israel will not negotiate with a Palestinian government backed by
> Hamas, a terrorist organization that calls for Israel's destruction.
> (Somfalvi, *Ynet News*, 24 April 2014)
>
> **"**

In response, Mahmoud Abbas said there was 'no incompatibility between reconciliation and the talks' (BBC News, 23 April 2014) and that the Palestinians were committed to peace. Within days of suspending talks Israel imposed economic sanctions against the Palestinians, cancelled plans to build homes for Palestinians in the West Bank and created new restrictions on Palestinian banking and freedom of movement.

'Operation Protective Edge' 2014

Following the agreement between Fatah and Hamas, and the breakdown of the US-brokered peace talks in April 2014, tensions were running high in the region. The kidnap and murder of three Israeli teens by a lone Hamas cell in June 2014 resulted in the arbitrary arrest and detention of over 350 Palestinians by Israel. This led to an increase in rocket attacks from the Gaza Strip into neighbouring Israeli territory in retaliation.

Most of the rockets were destroyed by Israel's 'Iron Dome' anti-missile system, though several Israeli civilians were killed and local infrastructure damaged. Israel responded with 'Operation Protective Edge', a combined air bombardment and ground assault designed to destroy Hamas's rocket facilities and the tunnels that fighters used to cross from the Gaza Strip into Israeli-held territory.

Over the course of the 50-day invasion, over two thousand Palestinians were killed and more than 100,000 were made homeless; this is the equivalent of nearly 10 per cent of the territory's population.

> **"**
>
> Gaza's electricity infrastructure, sewage pipes and agricultural land had taken a severe hit as well as 220 factories, 205 mosques, two of the three churches in Gaza, several TV stations and 10 hospitals which were badly damaged or destroyed.
>
> (Schulze, *The Arab–Israeli Conflict*, p. 114)
>
> **"**

	0 - 5 Years	Children	Women	Seniors	Men	Total
Palestinian	180	346	247	112	506	1,391
Israeli	1				5	6

(Source: *B'tselem*. Excludes Hamas fighters (765 fatalities) and members of the IDF (63 fatalities).

UN recognition of Palestine as a State

On 29 November 2012, the Palestinian cause took a major step forward when the UN General Assembly voted to grant Palestine non-member observer State status at the UN. The resolution on the status of Palestine in the UN was adopted by the 193-member General Assembly with a vote of 138 in favour to nine against, with 41 abstentions.

Mahmoud Abbas, the President of the Palestinian Authority, told the Assembly:

> **"**
>
> Your support for our endeavour today ... will send a promising message—to millions of Palestinians on the land of Palestine, in the refugee camps both in the homeland and the Diaspora, and to the prisoners struggling for freedom in Israel's prisons—that justice is possible and that there is a reason to be hopeful and that the peoples of the world do not accept the continuation of the occupation.
>
> (UN News Centre, 29 November 2012)
>
> **"**

Israel and its supporters were furious with this decision. Israel's Ambassador to the UN, Ron Prosor, said his delegation could not accept the resolution 'because this resolution is so one-sided, it doesn't advance peace, it pushes it backwards'.

Israel immediately sought to punish the Palestinians for the results of the General Assembly vote. A few days later, Israel seized tax revenues of more than US $120 million dollars from the Palestinian Authority. This decision was ethically and morally reprehensible; the funds belonged to the Palestinians and the seizure came in the midst of a severe economic crisis in the West Bank.

In his fury, Netanyahu implemented the E1 expansion plan for further illegal settlement building in the West Bank. The E1 expansion plan closed off East Jerusalem from the rest of the West Bank and further split the West Bank into two cantons, making the prospect of a contiguous Palestinian state impossible.

The US and Israeli settlement expansion

Although still regarded as Israel's unconditional ally, the US under the Obama administration had a complicated relationship with the right-wing administration of Benjamin Netanyahu.

In December 2016 Egypt introduced a resolution to the United Nations Security Council:

> **"**
>
> *Condemning* all measures aimed at altering the demographic composition, character and status of the Palestinian Territory occupied since 1967, including East Jerusalem, including, inter alia, the construction and expansion of settlements, transfer of Israeli settlers, confiscation of land, demolition of homes and displacement of Palestinian civilians, in violation of international humanitarian law and relevant resolutions.
> (United Nations, Security Council 7853rd Meeting, SC/12657, 23 December 2016)
>
> **"**

In order to be adopted, a Security Council resolution requires nine votes in favour and no vetoes by the permanent members (United States, France, Russia, Britain and China). This time, however, the resolution was passed by 14 votes with the US pointedly abstaining. The Israeli government was furious, and stated:

> **"**
>
> Israel rejects this shameful anti-Israel resolution at the UN and will not abide by its terms…The Obama administration not only failed to protect Israel against this gang-up at the UN, it colluded with it behind the scenes…Israel looks forward to working with president-elect Trump and with all our friends in Congress, Republicans and Democrats alike, to negate the harmful effects of this absurd resolution.
> (Beaumont, *The Guardian*, 23 December 2016)
>
> **"**

The consensus amongst political commentators was that the Obama administration was making a point to the incoming, right-wing, Trump administration: the only way to achieve lasting peace in the Middle East, and to resolve the Palestine–Israel conflict, was for Israel to start by suspending its continuing policy of land confiscation and building settlements. However, the immediate Israeli response, in direct contravention of the Security Council's resolution, was to pass the 'Law on the Regulation of Settlement in Judea and Samaria' in February 2017. This legislation retroactively legalized almost 4,000 homes built on Palestinian land.

Condemned by peace movements as making 'theft an official Israeli policy' (*Peace Now*, 7 February 2017), the law recognised thousands of illegally built Jewish settler homes constructed on privately owned Palestinian land. The insensitivity of passing this law was not lost on the international community. It was described as reflecting 'Israel's manifest disregard of international law' by Human Rights Watch (AFP, *Dawn*, 8 February 2017). Nicky Mladenov, the UN's special coordinator for the Middle East Peace Process, said the law would 'have far-reaching legal consequences for Israel and greatly diminish the prospects for Arab-Israeli peace' (Reed, *Financial Times*, 6 February 2017).

Mahmoud Abbas, the Palestinian President, said the law was 'contrary to international law', and emphasised that:

> **"**
>
> This is an aggression against our people that we will be opposing in international organisations…What we want is peace…but what Israel does is to work towards one state based on apartheid.
>
> (McKernan, *The Independent*, 7 February 2017)
>
> **"**

The faltering peace process

Donald Trump, throughout the US presidential campaign, had dismissed the support of a two-state settlement and rejected the idea that 'Israel is an occupier' of Palestinian lands. Trump also failed to condemn Israeli settlement expansion, commenting during his campaign that:

I think Israel should have—they really have to keep going. They have to keep moving forward…No, I don't think there should be a pause.

(*Haaretz*, 3 May 2016)

Approximately one week after the Regulation Law was passed, Benjamin Netanyahu had his first face-to-face meeting with President Trump.

Contrary to previous US presidents, Trump was vague and confused over whether to back a two-state solution to the Palestine–Israel question:

I'm looking at two-state and one-state, and I like the one that both parties like [laughter]. I'm very happy with the one that both parties like. I can live with either one… thought for a while the two-state looked like it may be the easier of the two. But honestly, if Bibi and if the Palestinians—if Israel and the Palestinians are happy, I'm happy with the one they like the best.

(Embury-Dennis, *The Independent*, 16 February 2017)

The Israeli government was encouraged by President Trump's comments, who had described Netanyahu as 'a smart man, great negotiator' in the same meeting. Israel was also encouraged by Trump's appointment of David Friedman, Trump's bankruptcy lawyer and an advisor on Israel during his election campaign, as the new US ambassador to Israel. Friedman was well known for his views on the Palestinian question: he 'opposes the two-state solution…and has talked openly about replacing it with a one-state model where Israel annexes the occupied West Bank' (Sanchez, *The Telegraph*, 16 December 2016).

> 66
>
> The rules of the game have changed with Donald Trump's arrival as president…We no longer have our hands tied as in the time of Barack Obama. Now we can finally build.
>
> (Meir Turgeman, Jerusalem's deputy mayor, quoted in Beaumont, *The Guardian*, 22 January 2017)
>
> 99

With Trump's pro-Israel position, the peace process has reached an impasse. The last meeting between the Palestinians and the Israelis took place in Washington in 2013. Since then life for the average Palestinian has comprised of checkpoints, harassment, humiliation, poverty and injustice.

> 66
>
> It is like being in a zoo…People just want to feel human and have a good life, like anywhere else.
>
> (Murad Wash, 34, quoted in Beaumont, *The Guardian*, 6 June 2017)
>
> 99

To punish the Palestinians, the Trump administration declared in 2018 it would stop the funding of the UN Relief and Works Agency (UNRWA), that provides basic humanitarian needs of over five million Palestinians refugees.

USA Embassy Move

One of the most detrimental obstacles to peace was the decision by the Trump administration in May 2018 to move the US embassy from Tel Aviv to Jerusalem. One year after the USA moved the embassy and Israel lobbying the world to follow suit only Guatemala has established an embassy in Jerusalem.

Trump: Settlements and Golan Heights

In November 2019, the Trump administration announced it will no longer abide by a 1978 State Department legal opinion that Israeli settlements were inconsistent with international law. The Trump administration's decision on settlements came at the back of an announcement in March 2019 that considers Israel's 1981 annexation of the occupied Golan Heights from Syria as legal.

Gaza Great March of Return

On 30 March 2018, Palestinians began a weekly Friday protest near the Israeli wall, east of the Gaza Strip. Palestinians are calling for the right of return to their homes in accordance with UN Resolution 194 and are demanding an end to the Israeli blockade of Gaza. In the one year of the Great March of Return from 30 March 2018 to 30 March 2019:

Israel has injured 28,939 Palestinians and killed 195 Palestinians, including 41 children.
(OCHA Protection of Civilians database).

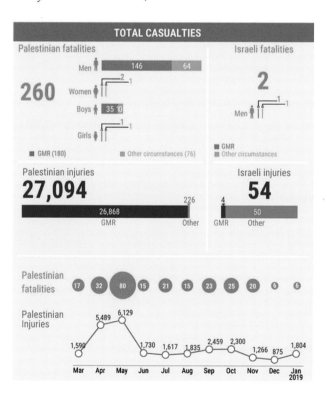

Source: OCHA United Nations Office for the Coordination of Humanitarian Affairs.

A United Nations inquiry into the Great March of Return has called to investigate Israeli use of lethal force against peaceful protesters and considered if Israeli actions may amount to war crimes.

Apartheid and Israel's nation-state law

On 19 July 2018, the Israeli parliament, the Knesset, adopted the racist legislation that defined Israel as "the historical homeland of the Jewish people and they have an exclusive right to national self-determination in it". The bill establishes Hebrew as the official language and considers "Jewish settlement as a national value".

Israel to be investigated for War Crimes

It is in the backdrop of the human rights abuses of Palestinians that an appeal was made by Palestinians to the International Criminal Court (ICC) to investigate Israel. In December 2019 the ICC announced it would launch a full investigation into alleged war crimes in Palestine by Israel.

CHAPTER 32

The Way Forward

The way forward is for Palestinians (Christians, Muslims and others) and Jews to live together in peace.

How can this be achieved?

The international community, whose concerns are for the just application of international law, human rights and world peace, must bring the two sides together. They must employ political, economic and diplomatic pressure to enforce a just and long-lasting peace, whereby future generations can live in harmony.

The way forward is to adopt the model of post-apartheid South Africa, and to create a single state where Jews and Palestinians can live and work together.

The Jews who have entered and occupied Palestinian land illegally would remain, but all Palestinian refugees must have a right of restitution and return; a council of truth and reconciliation must be formed and a 'true' democratic system established.

32.1 'Jews and Arabs refuse to be enemies': Aymen and Harsh meet at a protest in New York

> **A possible land solution**
> o Present Land Occupation: 78 per cent of Jews are concentrated in 15 per cent of 'Israeli territory'.
> o 75 per cent of the land is sparsely occupied.
> o In 2019, there are around 450,000 Israelis occupying the West Bank.
> o Even if all of the Palestinian refugees returned, the population to land ratio would only be raised minimally. It would most likely be counter-balanced by Jews who choose to leave of their own free will and the Palestinians who choose not to return.

The failure to attain one state is a political decision and not constrained by any other factor. The US and Britain, two countries that have supported the apartheid Zionist state need to be lobbied. They must be directed towards championing international law, the UN and Geneva Convention.

> **Nelson Mandela's solidarity with Palestine**
> No stranger to oppression, having been imprisoned for 27 years by the apartheid regime in South Africa, in 1997 Nelson Mandela called for Palestinian self-determination:
>
> 'I have come to join you today to add our own voice to the universal call for Palestinian self-determination and statehood…we know too well that our freedom is incomplete without the freedom of the Palestinians'
>
> (Mandela, Speech in Pretoria, 4 December 1997)

Facts & Figures

1. The Wall

The West Bank Separation Wall

In April 2002, a new phase of the illegal occupation began. The Israeli government approved the building of a wall deep into the West Bank. The Israelis claimed the wall was, to '[save] the lives of ... Israeli citizens who continue to be targeted by the terrorist campaign that began in 2000'. In reality, the result of the wall's construction has been the imprisonment and isolation of 25,000 Palestinians. The wall was built in several phases; the first two phases were completed in July 2003.

The Israeli apartheid wall, like the Great Wall of China, is visible from outer space. It is over 700 km long and 8 metres high secured with barbed wire, electric fences, trenches, security towers and electric sensors. By comparison, the Berlin Wall was only 155 km long and 3.6 metres high.

Facts about the Wall

o   Over 200,000 Palestinians living in 67 towns or villages suffer the direct impact of the wall.

o   Nearly 12,000 people from 16 villages are trapped between the wall and the Green Line (the 1967 border line).

o   At least 10 per cent of the West Bank has been illegally confiscated by Israel to build the wall, and Palestinians have not been compensated.

o   Tulkarm, Qalqiliya and East Jerusalem have been isolated from the rest of the West Bank by the wall.

o   Restrictions on freedom of movement caused by the wall has resulted in economic strangulation for thousands of Palestinians; it prevents Palestinians from reaching their own land and marketing their products across the West Bank.

o   Medical access has been significantly impaired as access for Palestinian villagers to hospitals has become extremely difficult.

o   Education has been denied to many as the wall lies between the homes of many teachers and the schools in which they teach. The wall is also a barrier for students reaching their schools.

o   The wall has meant a 10 km journey between Bidya and Salfit is now 80 km.

Qalqiliya: An Example

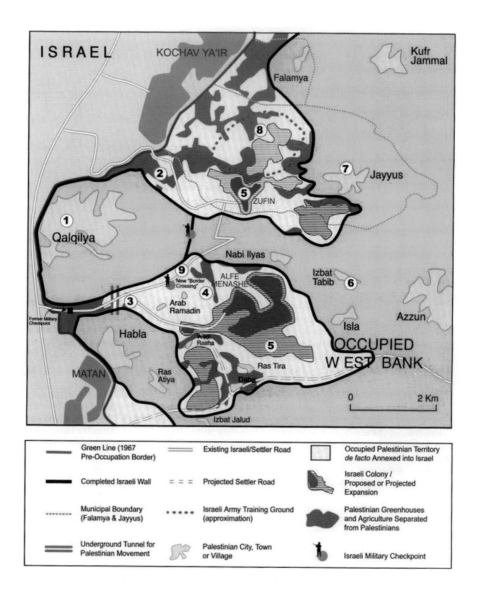

Legend:

Green Line (1967 Pre-Occupation Border)	Existing Israeli/Settler Road	Occupied Palestinian Territory de facto Annexed into Israel
Completed Israeli Wall	Projected Settler Road	Israeli Colony / Proposed or Projected Expansion
Municipal Boundary (Falamya & Jayyus)	Israeli Army Training Ground (approximation)	Palestinian Greenhouses and Agriculture Separated from Palestinians
Underground Tunnel for Palestinian Movement	Palestinian City, Town or Village	Israeli Military Checkpoint

This map shows the dramatic case of Qalqiliya, a town which is a prison in all but name. The wall has completely surrounded Qalqiliya, leaving only one opening guarded by two checkpoints. The city, once a flourishing centre of commerce, is suffocating.

What do Israel's allies say about the wall?

> "
> The wall would mean that a peace settlement
> is less likely and less possible.
> (Tony Blair, former British Prime Minister)
>
> The wall is a problem.
> (George W. Bush, former US President)
> "

In 1948 Israel occupied 78 per cent of Palestinian land, leaving just 22 per cent (the West Bank and Gaza) to the Palestinians. Since 1993 Palestinians have been demanding fair and unfettered ownership of just this 22 per cent.

Israel is taking additional land from the 22 per cent of mandate Palestine to build the wall. As a result the Palestinians have been pushed into around 12 per cent of their original homeland.

2. Restriction of movement

Perhaps the most harmful aspect to Palestinian human, civil, and economic rights has been Israel's policy of closure, in effect since March 1993, which severely restricts the Palestinians'' freedom of movement.

> "
> B'tselem (a leading Israeli human rights monitoring organisation),
> quotes senior officials from the Israeli Security Service who admit
> that closure of the West Bank contributes little to security. Instead,
> B'Tselem argues that closure, like curfew, serves primarily
> to destroy the Palestinian economy and society.
> (Brown, 'The Immobile Mass', p. 505)
> "

Palestinians queuing at an Israeli checkpoint

Israel's draconian closure policy, which denies Palestinians the freedom to travel freely between various areas and into Israel or Jerusalem, has crippled the Palestinian economy. In 2019, Palestinians found themselves in a much worse situation than in the days of Israeli Military Administration. In Gaza, 40 per cent of all households lived below the poverty line. According to the World Bank, the direct cost of Israel's closure to the Palestinian economy was over US $5 million per day.

Israel's arbitrary denial of Palestinians' right to travel from and to their homes in the West Bank, Gaza and East Jerusalem without obtaining permits is a clear violation of Article 13 of the Universal Declaration of Human Rights.

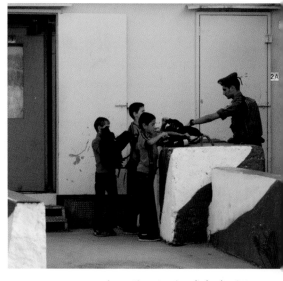

Inspection at an Israeli checkpoint

In addition, Israel's enforced closure policy represents a serious violation of religious freedom. This restriction prevents Muslims and Christians from reaching key holy sites and annual ritual events in Jerusalem and Bethlehem.

3. Deprivation of Water

Hydrological experts estimate that more than one third of all water used within Israel proper originates from aquifers in the West Bank. The Oslo Accords granted Israel veto power over Palestinian access to and use of crucial natural resources. Consequently, Palestinians in the West Bank and Gaza have suffered from severe water shortages.

Minimum Water Consumption Recommended by World Health Organisation	Israel	Palestinians
100 litres/day	600 litres/day	Average 60 litres/day (some consume only 20 litres/day)

A Palestinian boy collecting water

In practice, this means that whilst the Palestinians do not have drinking water, Israeli settlers bathe in freshwater swimming pools and water their lawns.

Today, the Israeli-owned Mekorot Water Company supplies dispossessed Palestinians with only 17 per cent of the underground water from their own land, which produces about 660 million cubic metres of water annually.

With desert land accounting for 60 per cent of Israel, 70 per cent of Syria, 85 per cent of Jordan, and 90 per cent of Egypt, it is indisputable that water resources will be a deciding factor in the achievement of peace or the outbreak of war in this volatile region.

4. Construction of illegal settlements

Israel's strategy of changing the Palestinian Occupied Areas is by creating 'facts on the ground'. This takes the form of building and expanding the illegal settlements and thus increasing the Jewish settler population in the West Bank.

Jewish settlements in the city of Ariel, West Bank

From 1967 to 2019 Israel has built 503 illegal settlements. 474 located in the West Bank and 29 in East Jerusalem.

In the first 100 days of 2000 Israel confiscated approximately 12,000 dunums of Palestinian land. In the month of April 2000 alone the Israeli authorities confiscated 1,956 dunums of land. In 2019, over 40 per cent of the West Bank is under settlement jurisdiction.

The impact of land confiscation has had disastrous social, economic, environmental and moral consequences on the Palestinians. The brutality of confiscation results in the loss of Palestinian social roots and also their main sources of income. Confiscation collectively punishes the Palestinian community and places on it unbearable social and economic pressures.

Palestinian woman trying to stop an Israeli bulldozer

5. Population of illegal Israeli settlers

In 2019, there were an estimated 664,500 illegal Israeli settlers in Occupied Palestine. 449,500 are in West Bank and 215,000 in East Jerusalem.

Illegal Israeli Settler Population in West Bank	
1967	0
1978	7800
1987	60300
1999	183,900
2009	296,700
2019	449,508

One of the main reasons for population growth within the occupied territories is that these areas are eligible for benefits and subsidies from the Israeli government. According to Ran Cohen, the Israeli Minister of Trade and Industry, 25 per cent of the Ministry's budget is spent in the West Bank settlements despite settlers representing just 2.5 per cent of Israel's population.

These figures do not, however, provide an accurate picture of the reality of Israeli settlement expansion within the occupied Palestinian territories. First, the population figures and numbers of housing units do not accurately reflect the scale of land expropriation.

GAZA STRIP 2003

EREZ CROSSING

GAZA

NETZARIM

(KARNI) CROSSING

DEIR AL BALAH

ISRAEL

KFAR DAROM

KISSUFIM CROSSING

KHAN YUNIS

GUSH KATIF SETTLEMENT

MORAG

RAFAH

SUFA CROSSING

GAZA AIRPORT

	Palestinian cities, Localities and Refugee Camps
	Palestinian Autonomous Area
	Israeli Settlements and areas under Israeli control
	Settlement access road patrolled by Israel
	Green Line

A Palestinian family struggling to live, with illegal Israeli settlements in the background

6. Desecration of Al-Aqsa sanctuary

In addition to the continued expropriation of land, Israeli authorities has presided over a marked increase in violations of the Al-Aqsa sanctuary. Desecrating the sanctity of Al-Aqsa has become an accepted phenomenon in mainstream Israeli society. The identities of those storming Al-Aqsa are diverse and include settlers, Zionist tourists, soldiers and Israeli politicians including Knesset members. Those who perpetrate these violations are not held to account by the Israeli authorities. A study conducted by Al-Aqsa Foundation for Endowment and Heritage revealed that Al-Aqsa

Jewish settlers with senior Rabbis storm Al-Aqsa sanctuary

mosque and its surrounding area was subjected to attacks and violations by approximately 5,000 Zionists during 2011 alone. The number of attacks increased significantly in 2019 with nearly 11,000 Zionists storming the Al-Aqsa sanctuary.

The attacks against the sanctuary range from physical attacks to plots threatening the sanctity of the holiest Muslim site in Jerusalem. Other inflammatory acts by Zionists include dancing, partying and drinking wine within the confines of the Al-Aqsa sanctuary. On 28 May 2012, a group of approximately 160 IDF soldiers hoisted a three-metre long Israeli flag inside the holy Al-Aqsa mosque and posed for photos with it.

Directly outside the Al-Aqsa sanctuary, Israel has embarked on a campaign to Judaise the area around the Muslim-owned Buraq ('Wailing') Wall and Buraq Square west of Al-Aqsa mosque. Millions of Israelis and foreign tourists visit the Buraq Wall every year. Many historic buildings and infrastructure have been destroyed to remove the Islamic character and history of the area, which is a daily target of the Israeli occupation. This is in addition to the destruction of the

Magharibi Quarter, which was destroyed by the occupation following the Six-Day War of 1967.

Concurrent with the increased violations of the Al-Aqsa sanctuary is an unprecedented Israeli military presence in Jerusalem. The Israeli authorities implement policies aimed at decreasing and hindering a Muslim presence in the Noble Sanctuary by implementing banning orders and restricting the access of certain age groups. Israeli occupation authorities also prevent millions of Palestinians from the West Bank and Gaza Strip from reaching occupied Jerusalem and from performing acts of worship in Al-Aqsa mosque. Those Muslims that are fortunate enough to visit the mosque are often the subject of harassment and brutality from occupying Israeli forces.

Military presence at Al-Aqsa sanctuary

Extremist groups named the 'Temple Mount' and 'Land of Israel Faithful Movement' are the most vociferous in calling for the destruction of Al-Aqsa. When Palestinians resist the extremism, the Israeli government imposes greater restrictions and punishes them. The tensions surrounding the Al-Aqsa compound prompted Jordan, a guardian of the Noble Sanctuary, to protest to the United Nations. In April 2016 UNESCO condemned Israel's policies around Al-Aqsa mosque and stated that it:

"

Deeply deplores the failure of Israel, the Occupying Power, to cease the persistent excavations and works in East Jerusalem particularly in and around the Old City…

Calls on Israel, the Occupying Power, to allow for the restoration of the historic Status Quo, that prevailed until September 2000, under which the Jordanian Awqaf (Religious Foundation) Department exercised exclusive authority on Al-Aqsa Mosque/Al-Haram Al-Sharif, and its mandate extended to all affairs relating to the unimpeded administration of Al-Aqsa Mosque/Al-Haram Al Sharif, including maintenance, restoration and regulating access…

Strongly condemns the Israeli aggressions and illegal measures against the freedom of worship and Muslims' access to their Holy Site Al-Aqsa Mosque/Al-Haram Al Sharif, and requests Israel, the Occupying Power, to respect the historic Status Quo and to immediately stop these measures…

Firmly deplores the continuous storming of Al-Aqsa Mosque/Al-Haram Al-Sharif by the Israeli right-wing extremists and uniformed forces, and urges Israel, the Occupying Power, to take necessary measures to prevent provocative abuses that violate the sanctity and integrity of Al-Aqsa Mosque/Al-Haram Al-Sharif.

(UNESCO, 'Item 19, Occupied Palestine')

"

7. Palestinians held as prisoners by Israel

According to Addemeer, more than 800,000 Palestinians have been arrested by Israel since 1967. This constitute almost 20% of the total Palestinian population in the occupied Palestinian territories. In addition Bet'Selem states from the beginning of 2015 to the end of July 2017, 3,909 administrative detention orders were issued.

Israel uses the label of Administrative detention to hold Palestinians as prisoners without informing them why they are being held or allowing them to stand public trial. Palestinians are routinely held for months or years without being of the reason for their detention. One Palestinian was held for 8 years under administrative detention.

PALESTINIANS IMPRISONED

1967–1987:	535,000
1987–1994 (First Intifada):	175,000
2000–2002 (first two years of Al-Aqsa Intifada):	12,000
May 2019:	4,787

8. Israel's assassination policy

Between 2000 and 2004, Israel assassinated 424 Palestinians, including Sheikh Ahmed Yassin and Abdul Aziz Rantisi. International law prohibits without exception the extrajudicial killing of occupied persons. Israel's policy of assassination is without doubt in contravention of International law, which constitutes a breach of the fourth Geneva Convention and is therefore subject to international criminal prosecution.

Demolition of a Palestinian home

9. House demolitions by Israel

There have been so many Palestinian homes demolished that it is impossible to provide an estimate of the destruction. In the first year of the Al-Aqsa Intifada alone (September 2001–September 2002) over 9,000 homes were demolished, making nearly 40,000 Palestinians homeless. According to the Israeli Committee Against House Demolitions (ICAHD), since 1967 Israel has demolished more than 28,000 Palestinian homes, businesses, livestock facilities and other structures. In 2019, 572 structures were demolished, displacing 819 people.

House demolitions are normally carried out early in the morning. Israeli troops seal off a village or street, bringing in bulldozers and surprising the unsuspecting victims. Palestinians are not given time to gather their belongings, and any attempts to resist are brutally subdued. When the demolition is complete (which invariably includes the destruction of the access road and uprooting of trees), the Israelis declare the area open once more.

10. Palestinians' loss of residency rights in East Jerusalem

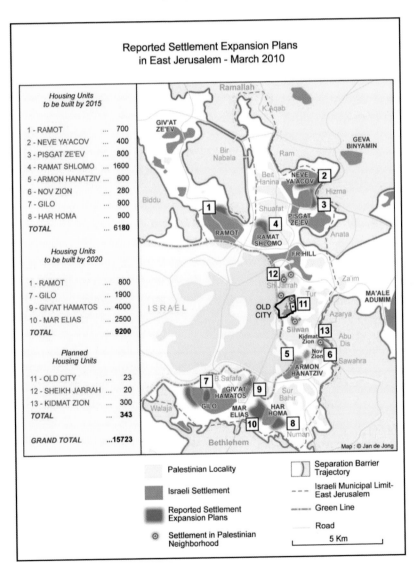

Since 1967, Israel has revoked the rights of nearly 15,000 Palestinians from residing in Jerusalem.

Israel's motive is to expand Jerusalem's boundaries to ensure that it retains control of this self-defined area of Jerusalem.

There has been a dramatic reduction of the Palestinian population within the Old City of Jerusalem, which contains the holiest Christian and Muslim sites. Zionist fundamentalists are forcing Christians and Muslims out of the city and are imposing their own mark by placing a Star of David on Palestinian homes occupied by Jewish settlers.

Star of David tagged on Palestinian doors

11. Building an 'Iron Ring' around Jerusalem

Israeli policy has been to flood Jerusalem with the Jewish population and to gradually push out the Palestinians, thereby creating a Jewish majority in Jerusalem. Israel is now continuing on all fronts with the Judaisation of Jerusalem. The old Christian and Islamic names of streets and historical sites, reflecting their heritage to Jerusalem, are being replaced with new Hebrew names.

Israeli/Jewish population (approx)	West Jerusalem	East Jerusalem
1967	198,000	-
1995	240,000	160,000
2019	300,000	230,000

Housing construction in East Jerusalem:

o   1992 – 3,116 units.

o   1993 – 2,720 units.

Peace Now found that in the period 1967 to 2019 Israel has issued 21,834 permits for housing units for Jewish settlements in east Jerusalem and just 9,536 for Palestinian neighbourhoods.

Global Palestinian refugee population (31 December, 2019)
Palestinians are the largest and longest suffering group of refugees in the world. One in three refugees world wide is Palestinian. There are about 7.2 million Palestinian refugees worldwide.

12. Jewish immigration into Palestine
(See graph on next page)

13. Land Confiscation
Before the 1948 War, Palestinians owned 87.5 per cent of the total land of Palestine, while Jews owned 6.6 per cent of the total land. The remaining 5.9 per cent was 'state land' as classified by the British Mandate (A Survey of Palestine, 1945–1946). In 2019 Israel has confiscated 88 per cent of the land.

14. Population of Christians in Palestine
At the beginning of the twentieth century, Christians composed over 20 per cent of the population. In 2019, they amounted to less than two per cent. According to the Palestinian Central Bureau of Statistics, in 2019 there are approximately 47,000 Palestinian Christians living in Palestine. In Jerusalem the Christian population is around 1.8 per cent at only 16,000.

Christians in Jerusalem	
1940	45,000
2019	16,000

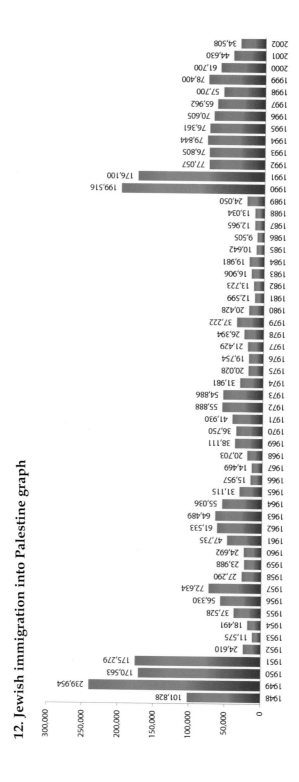

12. Jewish immigration into Palestine graph

Year	Immigration
1948	101,828
1949	239,954
1950	170,563
1951	175,279
1952	24,610
1953	11,575
1954	18,491
1955	37,528
1956	56,330
1957	72,634
1958	27,290
1959	23,988
1960	24,692
1961	47,735
1962	61,533
1963	64,489
1964	55,036
1965	31,115
1966	15,957
1967	14,469
1968	20,703
1969	38,111
1970	36,750
1971	41,930
1972	55,888
1973	54,886
1974	31,981
1975	20,028
1976	19,754
1977	21,429
1978	26,394
1979	37,222
1980	20,428
1981	12,599
1982	13,723
1983	16,906
1984	19,981
1985	10,642
1986	9,505
1987	12,965
1988	13,034
1989	24,050
1990	199,516
1991	176,100
1992	77,057
1993	76,805
1994	79,844
1995	76,361
1996	70,605
1997	65,962
1998	57,700
1999	78,400
2000	61,700
2001	44,630
2002	34,508

15. US aid to Israel 1949–1997

Israel's apartheid policies are financed and protected by the United States:

Foreign Aid grants and loans	US $72 billion
Other US aid (12.2 per cent of Foreign Aid)	US $9 billion
Interest to Israel from advanced payments	US $1.6 billion
Grand Total	US $85 billion
Total benefits per Israeli	US $14,630

o Most Americans are not aware of the amount of money that the US government sends to Israel. For the fiscal year ending 30 September 1997, the US gave Israel US $6.72 billion: US $6.194 billion fell under Israel's foreign aid allotment and US $526 million came from agencies such as the Department of Commerce, the US Information Agency and the Pentagon. The US $6.72 billion figure does not include loan guarantees and annual compound interest totalling US $3.122 billion that the US pays on money borrowed to give to Israel. It also does not include the cost to US taxpayers of IRS tax exemptions that donors can claim when they donate money to Israeli charities (donors claim approximately US $1 billion in federal tax deductions annually, which ultimately costs US taxpayers US $280–390 million).

o Total US aid to Israel is approximately one-third of the American foreign aid budget, even though Israel comprises of just 0.001 per cent of the world's population and already has one of the world's highest per capita incomes.

o Between 1949 and 2019, the US has given Israel a total of US $142.3 billion. Taking into account the interest costs borne by the US taxpayers, this means that the US government has given more federal aid to the average Israeli citizen in a given year than it has given to the average American citizen.

o In 2016, the U.S. and Israeli governments signed a new 10-year Memorandum of Understanding (MOU) on military aid, covering the period 2019 to 2028. Under the terms, the US pledges to provide $38 billion in military aid to Israel.

16. Chronology of Palestine

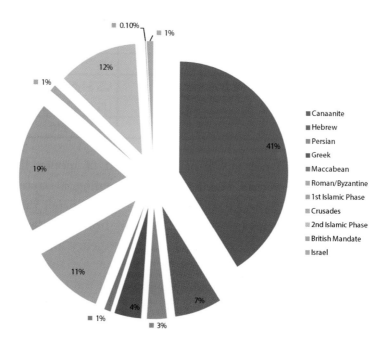

- Canaanite
- Hebrew
- Persian
- Greek
- Maccabean
- Roman/Byzantine
- 1st Islamic Phase
- Crusades
- 2nd Islamic Phase
- British Mandate
- Israel

17. Some of the UN resolutions against Israel

Resolution 57:	Expressing deep shock at the assassination of Count Bernadotte by Zionist terrorists.
Resolution 106:	Condemns Israel for Gaza raid.
Resolution 111:	Condemns Israel for raid on Syria that killed 56 people.
Resolution 127:	Recommends Israel to suspend its 'no-man's' zone in Jerusalem.
Resolution 162:	Urges Israel to comply with UN decisions.
Resolution 171:	Determines 'flagrant violations' by Israel in its attack on Syria.
Resolution 228:	Censures Israel for its attack on Samu in the West Bank, then under Jordanian rule.
Resolution 237:	Urges Israel to allow return of new 1967 Palestinian refugees.
Resolution 242:	Calls for withdrawal of Israel from territories occupied in the recent conflict.

Resolution 248:	Condemns Israel for its attack on Karameh in Jordan.
Resolution 250:	Calls on Israel to refrain from holding a military parade in Jerusalem.
Resolution 251:	'Deeply deplores' Israeli military parade in Jerusalem in defiance of resolution 250.
Resolution 252:	Declares 'invalid' Israel's acts to unify Jerusalem as Jewish capital.
Resolution 256:	Condemns Israeli raids on Jordan as 'flagrant violation'.
Resolution 259:	'Deplores' Israel's refusal to accept UN mission to probe occupation.
Resolution 262:	Condemns Israel for attack on Beirut airport.
Resolution 265:	Condemns Israel for air attacks in Jordan.
Resolution 267:	Censures Israel for administrative acts to change the status of Jerusalem.
Resolution 270:	Condemns Israel for air attacks on villages in southern Lebanon.
Resolution 271:	Condemns Israel's failure to obey UN resolutions on Jerusalem.
Resolution 279:	Demands withdrawal of Israeli forces from Lebanon.
Resolution 280:	Condemns Israel's attacks against Lebanon.
Resolution 285:	Demands immediate Israeli withdrawal from Lebanon.
Resolution 298:	Deplores Israel's changing of the status of Jerusalem.
Resolution 313:	Demands that Israel stop attacks against Lebanon.
Resolution 316:	Condemns Israel for repeated attacks on Lebanon.
Resolution 317:	Deplores Israel's refusal to release Arabs abducted in Lebanon.
Resolution 332:	Condemns Israel's repeated attacks against Lebanon.
Resolution 337:	Condemns Israel for violating Lebanon's sovereignty.
Resolution 347:	Condemns Israeli attacks on Lebanon.
Resolution 425:	Calls on Israel to withdraw its forces from Lebanon.
Resolution 427:	Calls on Israel to complete its withdrawal from Lebanon.
Resolution 444:	Deplores Israel's lack of cooperation with UN peacekeeping forces.
Resolution 446:	Determines that the Israeli settlements are a 'serious obstruction to peace' and calls on Israel to abide by the Fourth Geneva Convention.

Resolution 450:	Calls on Israel to stop attacking Lebanon.
Resolution 452:	Calls on Israel to cease building settlements in occupied territories.
Resolution 465:	Deplores Israel's settlements and asks all member states not to assist Israel's settlements programme.
Resolution 467:	'Strongly deplores' Israel's military intervention in Lebanon.
Resolution 468:	Calls on Israel to rescind illegal expulsions of two Palestinian mayors and a judge and to facilitate their return.
Resolution 469:	Strongly deplores Israel's failure to observe the council's order not to deport Palestinians.
Resolution 471:	Expresses deep concern at Israel's failure to abide by the Fourth Geneva Convention.
Resolution 476:	Reiterates that Israel's claims to Jerusalem are 'null and void'.
Resolution 478:	Censures (Israel) in the strongest terms for its claim to Jerusalem in its 'Basic Law'.
Resolution 484:	Declares it imperative that Israel readmit two deported Palestinian mayors.
Resolution 487:	Strongly condemns Israel for its attack on Iraq's nuclear facility.
Resolution 497:	Decides that Israel's annexation of Syria's Golan Heights is 'null and void' and demands that Israel rescind its decision forthwith.
Resolution 498:	Calls on Israel to withdraw from Lebanon.
Resolution 501:	Calls on Israel to stop attacks against Lebanon and withdraw its troops.
Resolution 509:	Demands that Israel withdraw its forces forthwith and unconditionally from Lebanon.
Resolution 515:	Demands that Israel lifts its siege of Beirut and allows food supplies to be brought in.
Resolution 517:	Censures Israel for failing to obey UN resolutions and demands that Israel withdraws its forces from Lebanon.
Resolution 518:	Demands that Israel cooperate fully with UN forces in Lebanon.
Resolution 520:	Condemns Israel's attack into West Beirut.

Resolution 573:	Condemns Israel 'vigorously' for bombing Tunisia in attack on PLO headquarters.
Resolution 587:	Takes note of previous calls on Israel to withdraw its forces from Lebanon and urges all parties to withdraw.
Resolution 592:	Strongly deplores the killing of Palestinian students at Bir Zeit University by Israeli troops.
Resolution 605:	Strongly deplores Israel's policies and practices denying the human rights of Palestinians.
Resolution 607:	Calls on Israel not to deport Palestinians and strongly requests it to abide by the Fourth Geneva Convention.
Resolution 608:	Deeply regrets that Israel has defied the United Nations and deported Palestinian civilians.
Resolution 636:	Deeply regrets Israeli deportation of Palestinian civilians.
Resolution 641:	Deplores Israel's continued deportation of Palestinians.
Resolution 672:	Condemns Israel for violence against Palestinians at the Haram Al-Sharif/Temple Mount.
Resolution 673:	Deplores Israel's refusal to cooperate with the United Nations.
Resolution 681:	Deplores Israel's resumption of the deportation of Palestinians.
Resolution 694:	Deplores Israel's deportation of Palestinians and calls on it to ensure their safe and immediate return.
Resolution 726:	Strongly condemns Israel's deportation of Palestinians.
Resolution 799:	Strongly condemns Israel's deportation of 413 Palestinians and calls for their immediate return.
Resolution 904:	Calls upon Israel, the occupying power, to take and implement measures, inter alia, the confiscation of arms, with the aim of preventing illegal acts of violence by settlers.
Resolution 1073:	Calls for the safety and security of Palestinian civilians to be ensured.
Resolution 1322:	Calls upon Israel to scrupulously abide by the Fourth Geneva Convention regarding the responsibilities of an occupying power.
Resolution 1402:	Calls for Israel to withdraw from Palestinian cities.
Resolution 1403:	Demands that Israel go through with the implementation of its resolution 1402, without delay.

Resolution 1405:	Calls for UN inspectors to investigate civilian deaths during an Israeli assault on the Jenin refugee camp.
Resolution 1435:	Calls on Israel to withdraw to positions of September 2000 and end its military activities in and around Ramallah, including the destruction of security and civilian infrastructure.

Bibliography

ABU TOAMEH, Khaled, 'Erekat: Peace Talks Have Failed, PA Should Seek Statehood Recognition', *The Jerusalem Post*, 30 December 2013. Available at http://www.jpost.com/Diplomacy-and-Politics/Erekat-Peace-talks-have-failed-PA-should-seek-statehood-recognition-336586 (accessed on 21 November 2017).

ABUKHATER, Maher, '20 Palestinians hurt in clashes with Israeli police at Al Aqsa holy site', *Los Angeles Times*, 13 September 2015. Available at http://www.latimes.com/world/middleeast/la-fg-police-palestinian-protesters-20150913-story.html (accessed on 22 November 2017).

ABU-SITTA, Salman, *The Palestinian Nakba, The Register of Depopulated Localities in Palestine*, London: The Palestinian Return Centre, 1998.

AFP, 'Israel settler law angers world powers, US silent', *Dawn*, 8 February 2017. Available at https://www.dawn.com/news/1313439 (accessed on 22 November 2017).

ALDERMAN, Geoffrey, 'An "invasion" that should not be repelled', *Jewish Chronicle*, 31 May 2002.

AL-NAIMI, A., *Al-Yahud wa al-Dawah al-Uthmaniyah*, 1998.

ARMSTRONG, Karen, *The Spirit of Palestine*. Edited by A. Duncan, et al., n. p., 1994.

AUB (American University of Beirut), 'College Hall', *Digital Documentation Center*, n.d. Available at http://ddc.aub.edu.lb/projects/tour/buildings/b14.html (accessed on 16 November 2017).

AVI-YONAH, Michael (ed.), *A History of the Holy Land*. Translated by C. Weiss and P. Fitton), New York: Macmillan, 1969.

BAMFORD, James, *Body of Secrets: How America's NSA and Britain's GCHQ Eavesdrop on the World*, London: Arrow Books, 2002.

BAR-ZOHAR, Michael, *Ben-Gurion; the Armed Prophet*, Englewood Cliffs, NJ: Prentice-Hall, 1968.

BBC NEWS, 'Hamas and Fatah unveil Palestinian reconciliation deal', 23 April 2014. Available at http://www.bbc.com/news/world-middle-east-27128902

(accessed on 21 November 2017).

BEAUCHAMP, Zack, 'Jerusalem's worrying al-Aqsa clashes, explained', *Vox*, 19 September 2015. Available at https://www.vox.com/2015/9/19/9354105/jerusalem-al-aqsa-clashes (accessed on 22 November 2017).

BEAUMONT, Peter, 'A day in the life of the West Bank occupation', *The Guardian*, 6 June 2017. Available at https://www.theguardian.com/world/2017/jun/06/a-day-in-the-life-of-the-west-bank-occupation (accessed on 22 November 2017).

BEAUMONT, Peter, 'Israel reveals plans for nearly 600 settlement homes in East Jerusalem', *The Guardian*, 22 January 2017. Available at https://www.theguardian.com/world/2017/jan/22/israel-reveals-plans-for-nearly-600-settlement-homes-in-east-jerusalem (accessed on 22 November 2017).

BEAUMONT, Peter, 'US abstention allows UN to demand end to Israeli settlements', *The Guardian*, 23 December 2016. Available at https://www.theguardian.com/world/2016/dec/23/us-abstention-allows-un-to-demand-end-to-israeli-settlements (accessed on 22 November 2017).

BEGIN, Menachem, *The Revolt: Story of the Irgun*, London: W.H. Allen, 1983.

BEN-GURION, David, *Rebirth and Destiny of Israel*, New York: Philosophical Library, 1954.

BLACK, Ian, Peter Beaumont and Dan Roberts, 'Israel suspends peace talks with Palestinians after Fatah-Hamas deal', *The Guardian*, 24 April 2014. Available at https://www.theguardian.com/world/2014/apr/24/middle-east-israel-halts-peace-talks-palestinians (accessed on 21 November 2017).

BLACK, M. (ed.), *Doten sifte yeshenim* (3 volumes), New York, 1959.

BONDS, J., Jimmy Emerman, Linda John, et al., *Our Roots are Still Alive*, San Francisco: Peoples Press, 1977.

BRAUN, Hanna, 'A Basic History of Zionism and its Relation to Judaism', Information Clearing House, September 2001. Available at http://www.informationclearinghouse.info/article4549.htm (accessed on 17 November 2017).

BRENNER, Lenni, *Zionism in the Age of Dictators*, Westport, CT: Lawrence Hill, 1983.

BROWN, Alison P., 'The Immobile Mass: Movement Restrictions in the West Bank', *Social & Legal Studies*, vol. 13, no. 4, 2004, pp 501–521. Available at http://citeseerx.ist.psu.edu/viewdoc/download?doi=10.1.1.901.4494&rep=rep1&type=pdf (accessed on 17 November 2017).

BUTLER, Alfred J., *The Arab Conquest of Egypt*, Oxford: Oxford University Press,

1978.

CARTER, Jimmy, 'President Obama can still advance Israeli/Palestinian peace', *USA Today*, 17 March 2016. Available at https://www.usatoday.com/story/opinion/2016/03/17/israel-palestine-peace-two-state-solution-jimmy-carter-obama-camp-david-column/81808662/ (accessed on 22 November 2017).

CATHOLIC ONLINE, 'Israel incensed as the Vatican recognizes the state of Palestine', 14 May 2015. Available at http://www.catholic.org/news/international/europe/story.php?id=60459 (accessed on 21 November 2017).

CHILDERS, Erskine B., 'The Other Exodus', *The Spectator*, 12 May 1961. Available at http://archive.spectator.co.uk/article/12th-may-1961/8/the-other-exodus (accessed on 16 November 2017).

CHOMSKY, Noam, *Masters of Mankind: Essays and Lectures, 1969–2013*, London: Penguin, 2015.

CHOMSKY, Noam, *The Fateful Triangle: The United States, Israel and the Palestinians*, London: Pluto Press, 1999.

COHEN, Michael, Palestine, *Retreat from the Mandate: The Making of British Policy, 1936–45*, London: Paul Elek, 1978.

DAVID, Ron, *Arabs and Israel for Beginners*, New York: Writers and Readers, 1993.

DAVIS, Uri, *Apartheid Israel: Possibilities for the Struggle Within*, London: Zed Books, 2003.

DUNCAN, Frederick and August C. Krey (eds), *Parallel Source Problems in Medieval History*, New York: Harper & Brothers, 1912.

EL FASSED, Arjan, 'Mandela's First Memo to Thomas Friedman' *The Electronic Intifada*, 29 March 2001. Available at https://electronicintifada.net/content/mandelas-first-memo-thomas-friedman/4826 (accessed on 15 November 2017).

EL FASSED, Arjan, 'Mandela's Memo', *ArjanElFassad*, 6 September 2002. Available at http://arjanelfassed.tumblr.com/post/431008597/mandela-memo (accessed on 15 November 2017).

EMBURY-DENNIS, Tom, 'Donald Trump's speech on Israeli-Palestinian conflict in full', *The Independent*, 16 February 2017. Available at http://www.independent.co.uk/news/world/americas/donald-speech-israel-palestine-in-full-benjamin-netanyahu-talks-two-state-solution-a7583421.html (accessed on 22 November 2017).

ERNST, Morris, *So Far So Good*, New York: Harper and Brothers, 1948.

EVRON, Boas, *Jewish State or Israeli Nation*, Bloomington, IN: Indiana University Press, 1995.

FINKELSTEIN, Norman G., *Image and Reality of the Israel-Palestine Conflict*, London: Verso, 1995.

GEANAKOPLOS, Deno John, *Byzantium: Church, Society and Civilization Seen Through Contemporary Eyes*, Chicago: University of Chicago Press, 1984.

GOLDMANN, Nahum, *The Jewish Paradox*. Translated by S. Cox, New York: Grosset & Dunlap, 1978.

GRAETZ, H., *History of the Jews* (6 volumes), Philadelphia, The Jewish Publication Society of Britain, 1891.

GREEN, Stephen J., *Taking Sides: America's Secret Relations with a Militant Israel*, London: Faber and Faber, 1984.

HAARETZ, 'Trump: Israeli Settlement Construction in West Bank Should "Keep Going"', Haaretz, 3 May 2016. Available at https://www.haaretz.com/world-news/u-s-election-2016/1.717730 (accessed on 22 November 2017).

HADAWI, Sami, *Bitter Harvest: A Modern History of Palestine*, Northampton, MA: Interlink Publishing Group, 1991.

HAMMOND, Jeremy R., 'Israel's attack on Egypt in June '67 was not "pre-emptive"', *Foreign Policy Journal*, 4 July 2010. Available at https://www.foreignpolicyjournal.com/2010/07/04/israels-attack-on-egypt-in-june-67-was-not-preemptive/ (accessed on 12 November 2017).

HARRIS, Nigel, *National Liberation*, London: I. B. Tauris, 1973.

HERZL, Theodor, *The Diaries of Theodor Herzl*. Edited by M. Lowenthal, London: Victor Gollancz, 1958.

HERZL, Theodor, *The Jewish State*. Originally translated by S. d'Avigdor, New York: Dover Publications, Inc., 1988. Available at https://www.gutenberg.org/files/25282/25282-h/25282-h.htm (accessed on 21 November 2017).

HERZL, Theodor, *The Jews' State: A Critical English Translation*. Translated by H. Overberg, Lanham, MD: Rowman and Littlefield, 1997.

HERZL, Theodor 'Letter from Theodor Herzl to Yussuf Zia Al-Khalidi, Mayor of Jerusalem', United Nations General Assembly, 3 September 1947. Available at https://unispal.un.org/DPA/DPR/unispal.nsf/c17b3a9d4bfb04c-985257b28006e4ea6/fb6dd3f0e9535815852572dd006cc607?OpenDocument (accessed on 16 November 2017).

HITTI, Philip K., *History of the Arabs: From the Earliest Times to the Present*, London: Macmillan Education Ltd., 1970.

HM GOVERNMENT, 'Aliens Bill', *Hansard*, 4th series, 1905, vol. 49, c. 155. Available at http://hansard.millbanksystems.com/commons/1905/jul/10/

aliens-bill#S4V0149P0_19050710_HOC_406 (accessed on 16 November 2017).

HM GOVERNMENT, 'House of Commons Debate on Gaza', *Hansard*, vol. 486, pt. 11, 12 January 2009. Available at https://publications.parliament.uk/pa/cm200809/cmhansrd/cm090112/debindx/90112-x.htm (accessed on 15 November 2017).

HM GOVERNMENT, 'House of Commons Debate on Palestine (Terrorist Activities)', *Hansard*, vol. 404 cc 2242–2244, 17 November 1944. Available at http://hansard.millbanksystems.com/commons/1944/nov/17/palestine-terrorist-activities (accessed on 16 November 2017).

HM GOVERNMENT, *A Survey of Palestine*, London: HM Stationery Office, 1945–1946.

HM GOVERNMENT, *Report by His Majesty's Government in the United Kingdom of Great Britain and Northern Ireland to the Council of the League of Nations on the Administration of Palestine and Trans-Jordan for the year 1931*, London, Stationary Office, 1931. Available at https://unispal.un.org/DPA/DPR/unispal.nsf/0/C2567D9C6F6CE5D8052565D9006EFC72 (accessed on 16 November 2017).

HRW (Human Rights Watch), 'Israel/Gaza: Israeli Airstrike on Home Unlawful', 7 December 2012. Available at https://www.hrw.org/news/2012/12/07/israel/gaza-israeli-airstrike-home-unlawful (accessed on 15 November 2017).

JOSEPHUS, Flavius, *The Jewish War*. Translated by G.A. Williamson, New York: Dorset Press, 1995.

KARMI, Ghada, and Eugene Cotran (eds), *The Palestinian Exodus 1948–1998*, Reading, UK: Ithaca Press, 1999.

KHALIDI, Walid, *Before Their Diaspora: A Photographic History of the Palestinians 1876–1948*, Washington, DC: Institute for Palestine Studies, 1984.

KIDRON, Peretz, 'Truth Whereby Nations Live'. In *Blaming the Victims: Spurious Scholarship and the Palestinian Question* by Said, Edward W. and Christopher Hitchens (eds), London: Verso, 2001.

KING, Henry Churchill, and Charles R. Crane, 'King–Crane report on the Near East', *Editor & Publisher*, vol. 55, no. 27, 2d section, 1922. Available at https://wwi.lib.byu.edu/index.php/The_King-Crane_Report (accessed on 16 November 2017).

LEWIS, Ori, 'Israel announces plans for building 1,400 settlement homes', *Reuters*, 10 January 2014. Available at https://www.reuters.com/article/us-palestinians-israel-settlements/israel-announces-plans-for-building-1400-settlement-homes-idUSBREA090KW20140110 (accessed on 21 November 2017).

MA'AN NEWS AGENCY, 'Vatican and Palestine sign historic accord', 26 June 2015. Available at http://www.maannews.com/Content.aspx?id=766168 (accessed on 21 November 2017).

MANDELA, Nelson, 'Address by President Nelson Mandela at the International Day of Solidarity with the Palestinian People', South African History Online, 4 December 1997. Available at http://www.sahistory.org.za/archive/address-president-nelson-mandela-international-day-solidarity-palestinian-people-pretoria-4- (accessed on 17 November 2017).

MANDELL, Neville J., *The Arabs and Zionism before World War I*, Berkeley: University of California Press, 1976.

MCKERNAN, Bethan, 'Israel votes to legalise wildcat settler homes dubbed "an aggression against the Palestinian people"', *The Independent*, 7 February 2017. Available at http://www.independent.co.uk/news/world/middle-east/israel-vote-retroactively-settler-homes-private-palestinian-land-legal-settlements-west-bank-a7566451.html (accessed on 22 November 2017).

MEYERHOF, Max, 'Thirty-Three Clinical Observations by Rhazes (Circa 900 A.D.)', *Isis* 23, 2 (1935), pp 321–372.

MILBANK, Dana, 'Pronouncing Blame on the Israel Lobby', *The Washington Post*, 29 August 2006. Available at https://www.washingtonpost.com/archive/politics/2006/08/29/pronouncing-blame-on-the-israel-lobby/34fd7807-dc31-4beb-b1f4-7186c7f8b949/?utm_term=.dade00de0b59 (accessed 15 November 2017).

MOLISAK, Alina, and Shoshana Ronen (eds), *The Trilingual Literature of Polish Jews from Different Perspectives: In Memory of I.L. Peretz*, Newcastle Upon Tyne: Cambridge Scholars Publishing, 2017.

MONTAGU, Lord Edwin Samuel, *Public Record Office*, Cab. 24/24, 23 August 1917. Available at http://www.jewishvirtuallibrary.org/montagu-memo-on-british-government-s-anti-semitism (accessed 16 November 2017).

MORRIS, Benny, *Righteous Victims: A History of the Zionist-Arab Conflict, 1881–1999*, London: John Murray, 1999.

NAKHLEH, Issa, *Encyclopaedia of the Palestine Problem: Israeli War Crimes Committed in Lebanon in 1978 and 1982*, New York: Intercontinental Books, 1991.

NETANYAHU, Benjamin, 'Netanyahu's AIPAC Speech: The Full Transcript' *Haaretz*, 4 March 2014. Available at https://www.haaretz.com/israel-news/1.577920 (accessed on 21 November 2017).

PAPPÉ, Ilan, 'What Really Happened 50 Years Ago', *The Link*, 31, no. 1, January–

March 1998. Available at http://ameu.org/getattachment/50a70223-a56f-4048-b240-7dabd0306678/Israeli-Historians-Ask-What-Really-Happened-5-(1).aspx (accessed on 16 November 2017).

PATAI, Rafael (ed.), *The Complete Diaries of Theodor Herzl* (5 volumes). Translated by H. Zohn, New York: Herzl Press, 1960.

PCHR (Palestinian Centre for Human Rights), 'Attempts to Rescue the al-Dalu Family Ongoing; Israeli Occupation Forces Destroy House over Its Residents', 19 November 2012. Available at http://pchrgaza.org/en/?p=1873 (accessed 15 November 2017).

PEACE NOW, 'Legalization Law Passes Its Second and Third Readings', *Peace Now*, 7 February 2017. Available at http://peacenow.org.il/en/legalization-law-passes-second-third-readings (accessed on 22 November 2017).

QUANDT, William B., Paul Jabber and Ann Mosely Lesch, *The Politics of Palestinian Nationalism*, Berkeley: University of California Press, 1973.

QUIGLEY, John, *Palestine and Israel: A Challenge to Justice*, Durham, NC: Duke University Press, 1990.

REED, John, 'New Israeli law retroactively legalises settlements', *Financial Times*, 6 February 2017. Available at https://www.ft.com/content/1c9ab626-ecb5-11e6-930f-061b01e23655 (accessed on 22 November 2017).

ROKACH, Livia, *Israel's Sacred Terrorism: A Study Based on Moshe Sharett's Personal Diary and Other Documents*, Belmont, MA: AAUG Press, 1986.

RUBINSTEIN, Aryeh, *The Return to Zion*, Jerusalem: Keter Books, 1974.

RUDORENNOV, Jodi, 'Hoisting Dead Children, Gazans Mourn Family Killed by Israeli Strike', *The New York Times*, 19 November 2012. Available at http://www.nytimes.com/2012/11/20/world/middleeast/gazans-mourn-dalu-family-killed-by-israeli-bomb.html (accessed on 15 November 2017).

RWB (Reporters Without Borders), 'RWB condemns air strikes on news media in Gaza city', 18 November 2012. Available at https://rsf.org/fr/node/23725 (accessed on 15 November 2017).

SAID, Edward W., *The Question of Palestine*, New York: Times Books, 1980.

SANCHEZ, Raf, 'Donald Trump's ambassador to Israel supports settlements and opposes two-state solution', *The Telegraph*, 16 December 2016. Available at http://www.telegraph.co.uk/news/2016/12/16/donald-trumps-pick-us-ambassador-israel-says-work-jerusalem/ (accessed on 22 November 2017).

SCHMEMANN, Serge, 'General's Words Shed a New Light on the Golan', *The New York Times*, 11 May 1997. Available at http://www.nytimes.

com/1997/05/11/world/general-s-words-shed-a-new-light-on-the-golan. html?scp=1&sq=Moshe%20Dayan%20Rami%20Tal&st=cse (accessed 16 November 2017).

SCHULZE, Kirsten E., *The Arab–Israeli Conflict*, London: Routledge, 2017.

SEGEV, Tom, *One Palestine, Complete: Jews and Arabs under the British Mandate*, New York: Henry Holt and Co., 2001.

SEGEV, Tom, *The Seventh Million: The Israelis and the Holocaust*, New York: Hill and Wang, 1994.

SHERWOOD, Harriet and Hazem Balousha, 'Gaza ceasefire: Israel and Palestinians agree to halt weeks of fighting', *The Guardian*, 27 August 2014. Available at https://www.theguardian.com/world/2014/aug/26/gaza-ceasefire-israel-palestinians-halt-fighting (accessed on 21 November 2017).

SHERWOOD, Harriet and Paul Lewis, 'Middle East peace talks under way', *The Guardian*, 30 July 2013. Available at https://www.theguardian.com/world/2013/jul/30/middle-east-peace-talks-under (accessed on 21 November 2017).

SKOLNIK, F. (Editor in Chief), *Encyclopaedia Judaica*, 2nd Edition, volume 2. Jerusalem: Keter Publishing House Ltd, 2007.

SLATER, Jerome, 'Ideology vs. The national interest: Bush, Sharon, and U.S. policy in the Israeli-Palestinian conflict', *Security Studies*, 12, 1, 2002, pp 164–206.

SOMFALVI, Attila, 'Sanctions and suspended talks – Israel responds to Palestinian reconciliation', Ynet News, 24 April 2014. Available at https://www.ynetnews.com/articles/0,7340,L-4513046,00.html (accessed on 21 November 2017).

STANGER, Cary David, 'A Haunting Legacy: The Assassination of Count Bernadotte', Middle East Journal, 42, 2, Spring 1988, pp 260–272.

TEKINER, Roselle, Samir Abed-Rabbo and Norton Mezvinsky (eds), *Anti-Zionism: Analytical Reflections*, Brattleboro, VT: Amana Books, 1988.

THATCHER, Oliver J., and Edgar H. McNeal (eds), *A Sourcebook for Mediaeval History*, New York: Scribners, 1905.

THOMPSON, Mark, 'BBC and the Gaza appeal', *BBC News, The Editors*, 24 January 2009. Available at http://www.bbc.co.uk/blogs/theeditors/2009/01/bbc_and_the_gaza_appeal.html (accessed 15 November 2017).

TUCHMAN, B., *Bible and Sword: England and Palestine from the Bronze Age to Balfour*, New York: Random House, 1984.

TURTLEDOVE, Harry (tr.), *The Chronicles of Theophanes: Anni Mundi 6095–6305*

(A.D. 602–813), Philadelphia: University of Pennsylvania Press, 1982.

UNESCO, 'Draft Decisions Recommended by Programme and External Relations Commission (PX): Item 19, Occupied Palestine', 199 EX/19, 14 April 2016. Available at https://unispal.un.org/DPA/DPR/unispal. nsf/0/478CB772EE6415A385257EF4005A8B44 (accessed 20 November 2017).

UNITED NATIONS, '194 (III). Palestine -- Progress Report of the United Nations Mediator', A/RES/194 (III), 11 December 1948. Available at https://unispal. un.org/DPA/DPR/unispal.nsf/0/C758572B78D1CD0085256BCF0077E51A (accessed 16 November 2017).

UNITED NATIONS, 'General Assembly grants Palestine non-member observer State status at UN', *UN News Centre*, 29 November 2012. Available at http://www.un.org/apps/news/story.asp?NewsID=43640#.WgXRMdN-qM8 (accessed 15 November 2017).

UNITED NATIONS, 'Israel's Settlements Have No Legal Validity, Constitute Flagrant Violation of International Law, Security Council Reaffirms', Security Council 7853rd Meeting, SC/12657, 23 December 2016. Available at https://www.un.org/press/en/2016/sc12657.doc.htm (accessed on 22 November 2017).

UNITED NATIONS, 'Progress Report of the United Nations Mediator on Palestine Submitted to the Secretary-General for Transmission to the Members of the United Nations', Third Session, Supplement No. 11 (A/648), 16 September 1948. Available at https://unispal.un.org/DPA/DPR/unispal.nsf/0/AB14D4AAFC4E1BB985256204004F55FA (accessed 17 November 2017).

UNITED NATIONS, 'Resolution 242 (1967)', S/RES/242 (1967), 22 November 1967. Available at https://unispal.un.org/DPA/DPR/unispal. nsf/0/7D35E1F729DF491C85256EE700686136 (accessed 16 November 2017).

UNITED NATIONS, 'The situation in the Middle East', A/RES/37/123, 16 December 1982. Available at http://www.un.org/documents/ga/res/37/a37r123.htm (accessed 16 November 2017).

UNITED NATIONS, Resolution 521 (1982), *Open Documents*, 19 September 1982. Available at https://documents-dds-ny.un.org/doc/RESOLUTION/GEN/NR0/435/45/IMG/NR043545.pdf?OpenElement (accessed 16 November 2017).

UNIVERSITY OF MARYLAND, 'President Sadat's speech to the Knesset', Anwar Sadat Chair for Peace and Development, n.d. Available at https://sadat.umd.edu/sites/sadat.umd.edu/files/President%20Sadat%E2%80%99s%20Speech%20to%20the%20Knesset.compressed.pdf (accessed on 16 November

2017).

USHER, Graham, *Dispatches from Palestine: The Rise and fall of the Oslo Peace Process*, London: Pluto Press, 1999.

WEITZ, Yehiam, 'Jewish Refugees and Zionist Policy during the Holocaust', *Middle Eastern Studies*, 30, no. 2, 1994.

WHEATCROFT, Geoffrey, *The Controversy of Zion: Jewish Nationalism, the Jewish State, and the Unresolved Jewish Dilemma*, Reading, MA: Addison-Wesley Publishing, 1996.

WHITTING, Phillip (ed.), *Byzantium: An Introduction*, Oxford: Basil Blackwell, 1971.

WRIGHT, Clifford A., *Facts and Fables: The Arab-Israeli Conflict*, London: Routledge, 2015.

WRIGHT, Thomas (ed.), *Early Travels in Palestine*, New York: Dover Publications, 2003.

YALE LAW SCHOOL, 'British White Paper of 1939', *The Avalon Project*, n.d. Available at http://avalon.law.yale.edu/20th_century/brwh1939.asp (accessed on 16 November 2017).

YALE LAW SCHOOL, 'British White Paper of June 1922', *The Avalon Project*, n.d. Available at http://avalon.law.yale.edu/20th_century/brwh1922.asp (accessed on 16 November 2017).

ZAGOREN, Ruby, *Chaim Weizmann: First President of Israel*, Champaign, IL: Garrard Publishing Co., 1972.

ZANGWILL, Israel, 'The Return to Palestine', *New Liberal Review*, 2, no. 11 (December 1901), pp 615.

ZANGWILL, Israel, *The Voice of Jerusalem*, London: William Heinemann, 1920.

ZWEIG, Ronald, *Britain and Palestine during the Second World War*, Martlesham, Suffolk: Boydell Press, 1986.

Index